The Permanent Husband

*A Gripping Tale of Betrayal, Guilt,
and the Burden of the Past*

A Modern Translation

Adapted for the Contemporary Reader

Fyodor Dostoevsky

Table of Contents

Preface - Message to the Reader

Rebuilding the Greatest Library in Human History

Thousands of years ago, the Library of Alexandria was the heart of global knowledge — a sanctuary where the wisdom of every known civilization was gathered and shared freely.

And then, it was lost.

Now, we're rebuilding it — and you are invited to join us.

At the Library of Alexandria, we've set out to make every book available to *every person on Earth* — not just in print, but in every language, every format, and for every reader.

Here's how we do it:

- **Deluxe Print Editions at True Printing Cost** - Order any book as a high-quality paperback, elegant hardcover, or stunning boxset — and only pay what it costs to print. No markups. No middlemen.
- **Unlimited Access to the Greatest Works** - Enjoy thousands of timeless classics — from Plato to Shakespeare to Tolstoy — in beautiful, modern eBook and audiobook editions. Read and listen without limits — for every reader, everywhere.
- **Modern Translations for Every Language & Dialect** - We're reimagining the classics in clear, accessible language — and translating them into every dialect imaginable. Everyone deserves to understand humanity's greatest ideas.

When you visit **LibraryofAlexandria.com**, you're not just accessing books — you're joining a global movement to restore, preserve, and share the wisdom of civilization.

Join us today at LibraryofAlexandria.com

Together, we'll ensure the light of human wisdom never fades again.

With gratitude,
The Modern Library of Alexandria Team

Visit:

www.libraryofalexandria.com

Or scan the code below:

Introduction

Dostoevsky's Forgotten Masterpiece:
A Brief but Haunting Psychological Portrait

The Permanent Husband (also translated as The Eternal Husband) is one of the more compact yet piercing psychological novellas penned by Fyodor Dostoevsky, first published in 1869. While it lacks the epic scale of The Brothers Karamazov or Crime and Punishment, this work encapsulates much of the intense psychological insight, moral ambiguity, and darkly ironic tension for which Dostoevsky is renowned. At its core, The Permanent Husband explores the complex emotional terrain of guilt, revenge, pride, and the unresolved tensions of relationships marked by betrayal and humiliation.

This novella begins as a seemingly straightforward tale of a widower, Velchaninov, who finds himself unexpectedly confronted by Trusotsky—the husband of a woman with whom Velchaninov had once had an affair. What unfolds from this point, however, is a nuanced and shifting psychological battle between two men—one haunted by guilt and the other by shame—where the roles of victim and aggressor are continually reversed and destabilized.

In a broader literary context, this work sits at the crossroads of Dostoevsky's mature fiction. It reflects the philosophical and existential preoccupations that dominate his later works, while also drawing on the intense personal experiences and moral dilemmas that shaped his life. This introduction will explore the major themes, characters, and historical context of The Permanent Husband, and show how, despite its brevity, it belongs firmly among Dostoevsky's most significant psychological achievements.

Psychological Combat and
the Tragedy of the Ordinary Man

From the moment Trusotsky enters the scene, the novella presents a subtle but ferocious psychological duel. Dostoevsky masterfully builds tension not through grand plot twists but through the emotional instability of his characters. Both Velchaninov and Trusotsky are deeply flawed men, trapped by their own past actions and unable to move beyond them. The dramatic tension arises from the ambiguity of their confrontation: is it an attempt at revenge, reconciliation, self-punishment, or something far more chaotic?

Trusotsky is one of Dostoevsky's most fascinating creations. He is pathetic yet strangely menacing, passive yet capable of emotional cruelty. Described as timid and ridiculous—hence his name, which evokes the Russian word for coward—Trusotsky initially seems to be a man defeated by life. Yet his ability to humiliate Velchaninov, to unsettle him with eerie calmness, turns him into a strange mirror image of the protagonist. The more Velchaninov tries to assert control over the situation or recover his dignity, the more he becomes entangled in Trusotsky's unpredictable behavior. The result is a power dynamic that is constantly shifting, which reflects the novella's central concern: the impossibility of clearly separating guilt from victimhood, or justice from cruelty.

Velchaninov himself is a quintessential Dostoevskian figure—introspective, self-lacerating, and morally ambiguous. Once a rakish libertine, he is now middle-aged and marked by regret. His affair with Trusotsky's wife is long over, but the consequences remain like a shadow. When Trusotsky unexpectedly reappears in his life, bringing with him his young daughter Liza (whom Velchaninov suspects might be his own illegitimate child), the emotional fallout is immediate. Velchaninov's attempts to do the right thing are tinged with selfishness, superiority, and an inability to fully grasp the pain of others. Even his moments of compassion or self-reflection seem contaminated by vanity and uncertainty.

The relationship between these two men is less a clear narrative arc and more a sustained psychological disturbance. Each man becomes both torturer and victim, and their interactions feel like a dance of mutual obsession. What makes the novella so powerful is that Dostoevsky never offers a definitive resolution. The story ends with ambiguity, a sense that neither man has truly won or found peace, and that the past continues to echo in their lives.

This uncertain, almost nihilistic conclusion challenges the reader to consider how the burdens of the past—particularly guilt, betrayal, and humiliation—can corrode not only our relationships but our very sense of identity. Unlike traditional revenge narratives, The Permanent Husband offers no catharsis. Its brilliance lies in this refusal to comfort or resolve, in its ability to dramatize the unresolved trauma that persists in ordinary human interactions.

The Historical and Biographical Landscape Behind the Novella

To better understand The Permanent Husband, it's essential to consider its historical and personal context. The 1860s were a transformative period for Dostoevsky. After enduring a mock execution, ten years of Siberian exile, and financial ruin, he returned to the literary scene with a renewed focus on existential and spiritual themes. His second marriage to Anna Grigoryevna in 1867 brought some emotional stability, but his life continued to be marked by gambling addiction, epilepsy, and debt. These personal struggles deeply informed his fiction.

The themes of shame, moral compromise, and psychological torment in The Permanent Husband can be seen as reflections of Dostoevsky's own tormented conscience and precarious life. In many ways, Velchaninov's self-accusations and Trusotsky's pitiful dignity mirror Dostoevsky's recurring preoccupations: the difficulty of true repentance, the elusiveness of justice, and the endless capacity of the human soul to deceive itself.

The novella also responds to broader social and intellectual currents in 19th-century Russia. During the 1860s, Russian society was undergoing seismic shifts—serfdom had been abolished in 1861, radical political ideologies were gaining popularity, and traditional religious values were being questioned. Dostoevsky, while deeply critical of liberal and socialist movements, was also skeptical of the decaying aristocracy and the moral emptiness of Western materialism. His fiction during this period becomes a site for these conflicts to play out in the lives of his characters.

In The Permanent Husband, these tensions are more implicit than in works like The Devils or Notes from Underground, but they are no less present. The characters are caught between old values and modern desires, between social respectability and private vice. Trusotsky, in particular, represents the tragedy of the "little man" in Russian literature—a character type that had been popularized by Gogol and further developed by Dostoevsky. Powerless, ridiculous, and ignored by society, he nevertheless becomes the vehicle for profound psychological and moral inquiry.

Additionally, the novella should be read in light of Dostoevsky's interest in Christian themes of suffering, humility, and redemption. Although The Permanent Husband is less overtly theological than some of his longer works, the spiritual questions are never far from the surface. Can guilt purify or only corrode? Is forgiveness possible, or does it merely conceal pride and hypocrisy? Dostoevsky does not answer these questions directly, but he makes them felt in every interaction, every gesture, every ambiguous silence between his characters.

The Enduring Relevance of The Permanent Husband

Why does The Permanent Husband still matter today? In part, because it strips human relationships down to their most painful and awkward truths. It exposes the ways in which unresolved guilt and long-standing emotional wounds can distort even our best intentions. In an era where public discourse often reduces people to clear categories—villain or victim, hero or traitor—Dostoevsky reminds us that real human beings are infinitely more complicated. His characters are messy, contradictory, wounded, and often both sympathetic and repellent in the same breath.

The novella also speaks to the psychological cost of repression. Velchaninov has tried to bury the past, but it returns in the form of Trusotsky—not as a figure of wrath but as a constant, inescapable reminder of his moral failure. Trusotsky, for his part, is consumed by shame and longing, unable to express either clearly. Together, they enact a drama that feels almost claustrophobic in its emotional intensity, yet it resonates with anyone who has ever struggled with regret, pride, or the fear of truly confronting another human being.

For modern readers, The Permanent Husband offers an intensely relatable glimpse into the complexities of male ego, emotional vulnerability, and interpersonal dysfunction. It's a text that invites close reading, not because of a twisting plot, but because of the depth of emotional subtext. Dostoevsky doesn't give us answers—he gives us questions that disturb and linger.

This modern translation aims to retain the richness of Dostoevsky's voice while making his prose more accessible to contemporary readers. While preserving the psychological subtlety and narrative tension, this version removes some of the 19th-century linguistic density that can make Dostoevsky's shorter works feel more opaque than his longer ones. The goal is not simplification but clarity—to illuminate the brilliance of the original without losing its bite.

In conclusion, The Permanent Husband may be short, but it is not slight. It is a study in emotional paralysis, moral ambiguity, and the haunting persistence of the past. It reveals, in miniature, everything that makes Dostoevsky one of the most profound chroniclers of the human soul. Whether you are a longtime admirer of his work or a first-time reader, this novella will leave you unsettled, provoked, and—most importantly—changed.

Chapter 1

Summer had arrived, and Velchaninoff, contrary to his plans, was still in St. Petersburg. His trip to southern Russia had fallen through, and the business that kept him in the city seemed never-ending.

This business, which involved a lawsuit over property, had taken an unpleasant turn. Just three months earlier, the matter had seemed straightforward—there had been little doubt about who was in the right. But everything had suddenly changed.

"Everything else in my life seems to be falling apart too," Velchaninoff often muttered to himself.

He had hired a talented and well-known lawyer, though an expensive one. But Velchaninoff, impatient and mistrustful, started interfering in the case himself. He read and wrote documents—most of which the lawyer immediately discarded—visited court offices regularly, asked endless questions, and created confusion for everyone involved. At least, that's what his lawyer claimed when he begged Velchaninoff to leave town and get some rest in the countryside.

But Velchaninoff couldn't bring himself to leave. He stayed in the city, enduring its dust, stifling summer nights, and suffocating air—all things that were enough to destroy anyone's nerves. He had recently rented lodgings near the Great Theatre, but he didn't like them. Nothing seemed to go right for him. His hypochondria grew worse with each passing day, a condition he had struggled with for a long time.

Velchaninoff was a man who had seen much of the world. He was not young anymore—thirty-eight or perhaps thirty-nine years old—and he often lamented how this "old age," as he called it, had snuck up on him unexpectedly. However, he understood that his aging was more about the weight of his experiences than the number of years he had lived. If his ailments were creeping up on him, he believed they came from within rather than external causes. He still looked young. He was tall and sturdy, with thick, light brown hair untouched by gray, and a light beard that reached halfway down his chest. At first glance, he might seem easygoing or carefree, but a closer look revealed a man who was meticulous about proper behavior and who had been raised with the manners and grace of the finest society.

His manners were polished—relaxed yet elegant—despite his recent tendency to grumble and complain about nearly everything. He still carried himself with the kind of aristocratic confidence that likely even he didn't fully realize he had. Though intelligent, clever, and even talented, he remained blind to this trait. His healthy-looking face was marked by an almost feminine delicacy, a feature that had always drawn attention from women. He had large blue eyes, which ten years earlier had been full of charm and mischief, easily winning over anyone he wished to impress. But now, as he neared forty, their warmth and openness had faded. In their place was a cynical, cunning, and often ironic look. Recently, a new expression—a mix of sadness and pain, hard to define but deeply felt—had begun to appear, especially when he was alone.

It was a strange transformation. Just a few years ago, Velchaninoff had been a cheerful, carefree man, known for his unmatched ability to tell funny stories. Now, he preferred solitude above all else. He planned to distance himself from most of his friends, though this was unnecessary even with his current financial troubles. His vanity was likely to blame for this decision—he couldn't stand for his old friends to see him in his current state. With his proud and suspicious nature, the thought was unbearable.

In solitude, Velchaninoff's vanity began to change. It didn't diminish; instead, it transformed into a new kind of vanity, different from what he had known before. This new vanity focused on what he called "higher causes," though he sometimes wondered if there really were such things as higher and lower motives in life.

He described these "higher things" as matters he couldn't laugh at or ridicule when they happened in his private thoughts. Of course, it was a different story in social settings—there, he would be the first to dismiss or mock the same ideas. But alone, he couldn't bring himself to ridicule them. Yet, if he joined others, he would abandon those private resolutions and laugh them off.

Often, when he got up in the morning, he felt embarrassed by the thoughts and emotions that had consumed him during the long, sleepless nights—and recently, his nights had been restless. He became suspicious of everything and everyone, no matter how big or small, and he even started to doubt himself.

One thing was clear: during those sleepless nights, his thoughts and opinions changed drastically, sometimes becoming the complete opposite of what he believed during the day. This shift startled him, so he decided to consult a doctor he knew. He spoke casually, as though joking, but the doctor explained that this phenomenon was well-known to science. It was common for people with strong intellects and deep emotions to experience such changes during sleepless nights. The doctor added that sleeplessness often caused people to question lifelong beliefs or make life-changing decisions. He mentioned that in severe cases, this could become a disorder, requiring lifestyle changes, a healthier diet, or even travel to improve one's condition.

Velchaninoff stopped listening after that, but he became convinced that he was indeed suffering from some kind of illness.

Soon, his thoughts during the mornings began to resemble those of the night, but they were even harsher. Memories of his past started flooding back more vividly than ever. These memories came to him suddenly, without any apparent reason—events from ten or fifteen years ago, some so distant that he was amazed he could recall them at all.

But it wasn't just the memories themselves that troubled him. After all, anyone who has lived a full life has countless memories of the past. The issue was how these memories now seemed to take on a completely new meaning. He saw them in an entirely different light, as though from a perspective he had never considered before. Why did some of his actions now seem like crimes? This judgment didn't come from his mind alone—he wouldn't have trusted it if that were the case. Instead, his entire being condemned him. He found himself cursing his past and even weeping over it. A few years ago, if someone had told him he would cry about anything, he would have laughed at the idea.

At first, he recalled the unpleasant moments in his life: failures in social situations and humiliations. He remembered how someone had maliciously ruined his reputation, leading him to be asked not to visit a certain house anymore. He recalled a time, not so long ago, when he had been insulted in public and hadn't responded with a challenge. He thought about how a witty remark had been made at his expense during a gathering of charming women, and he hadn't been able to think of a reply. He also remembered unpaid debts and how he had foolishly squandered two respectable fortunes.

Then he began to recall memories of a more serious nature. He remembered insulting a poor, elderly clerk once. The man had covered his face with his hands and cried, and Velchaninoff had found it funny at the time. Now, he saw it in a completely different light. He also remembered how, just for fun, he had started a scandal about the young, beautiful wife of a schoolmaster. The husband eventually heard the rumors. Velchaninoff had left the town soon after and never found out how it ended, but now he began imagining the possible consequences of his actions. He couldn't stop his thoughts from

12

spiraling until another memory hit him—this time of a poor girl he had betrayed. He had been ashamed of her, never truly loved her, and had abandoned her and their child when he left St. Petersburg. Later, he searched for them both for an entire year but never found them.

Unfortunately, there were far too many memories like these, and each one seemed to drag along even more painful recollections. His vanity began to suffer under the weight of these memories. As mentioned before, his vanity had taken on a new form. There were rare moments now when he wasn't ashamed of no longer owning a carriage or being seen in shabby clothes by an old friend. Sometimes, even if one of these acquaintances looked at him with contempt, he could muster the strength to suppress any reaction. These moments of rising above himself were few, but they marked a shift. His vanity was no longer tied to his appearance or status. Instead, it focused on one nagging question that haunted his thoughts.

"There must be some power," he would think bitterly, "somewhere, that's obsessed with my morals and keeps sending me these awful memories and feelings of guilt! Fine, let them come—I don't care! They don't change a thing about me. I'm spineless, even at my miserable age of forty. If I thought I could gain something by starting another scandal, say, about that schoolmaster's wife, I wouldn't hesitate. I'd spread the rumor in an instant without a second thought."

Though he never had the chance to act on such an impulse again, just the thought that he would seize the opportunity if it arose was almost unbearable. Still, he wasn't tormented by guilt every moment of the day. There were times when he could breathe and rest from these memories. But the longer he stayed in St. Petersburg, the more unpleasant life became for him. By July, he was tempted to give up on his lawsuit altogether and leave for Crimea. But after an hour or so, he would scoff at the idea and mock himself for considering it.

"These thoughts won't go away just because I travel south," he told himself. "Once they start bothering you, there's no running from them. Besides, if my conscience is clear, why should I be scared of memories from the past?"

"Why should I leave at all?" he continued, sinking into a gloomy sort of reflection. "This city is perfect for someone like me—dust, heat, and this dreadful house. Add to that the ridiculous pomp and pretense of all those little 'civil servants' I deal with in the offices! Everyone here is so blunt and shameless, and that honesty deserves respect, I suppose. No, I won't leave. I'll stay here and die rather than run away!"

Chapter 2

It was the third of July, and the heat and humidity had become unbearable. Velchaninoff had spent the day rushing around, walking and driving without rest. He still had an evening visit planned to a state councillor who lived near the Chornaya Riéchka, or Black Stream, a visit he intended to make unannounced.

At six o'clock, he left his house again and headed to a restaurant on the Nefsky near the police bridge. It wasn't a fancy place, but it was French. He sat down in his usual corner, ordered his usual meal, and waited.

He always stuck to a one-rouble dinner, with wine paid for separately, which he considered a reasonable concession to the financial difficulties he was facing.

Each time, he would go through the same routine of wondering how he could possibly eat "such awful food," only to devour every bite with an appetite that made it seem as though he hadn't eaten in three days.

"This kind of appetite can't be healthy," he sometimes muttered to himself, noticing how voraciously he ate.

This time, though, he sat down in a terrible mood. He threw his hat angrily onto a nearby seat, leaned back in his chair, and brooded.

He was so irritable that the smallest annoyance—a neighbor rattling a plate, the waiter making a small mistake, or any other minor disruption—might set him off. He felt ready to shout or even cause a scene over the slightest thing.

The soup was served. He picked up his spoon and was about to start eating when he suddenly put it down and jumped up from his seat. A sudden thought struck him, and he instantly realized why he had been feeling so gloomy and unsettled over the past few days. For some reason, the truth seemed to dawn on him all at once. He stood there, everything becoming as clear as day.

"It's that hat!" he muttered. "It's all because of that stupid round hat with the crape band around it! That's the reason for all my trouble these last few days!"

He began to think, and the more he thought, the more uneasy he became. The significance of "the hat" seemed stranger and stranger to him.

"But wait—there's no significance!" he growled to himself. "What significance could there be? Nothing's even happened!"

The truth was this: about two weeks ago, near the corner of the Podiacheskaya, he had passed a man wearing a hat with a crape band. There was nothing particularly noteworthy about the man—he looked like anyone else—but as the man walked by, he stared at Velchaninoff so intensely that it was impossible not to notice him. Velchaninoff had even stopped to watch him for a moment.

Something about the man's face felt familiar, as though Velchaninoff had seen him before, though he couldn't recall where or when.

"But I've seen thousands of faces in my life," Velchaninoff thought. "I can't possibly remember them all!"

So he had continued on his way. By the time he had walked another twenty steps, it seemed as though he had forgotten all about the encounter, despite the strong impression it had made on him at first.

And yet, he hadn't truly forgotten. The impression stayed with him all day, and it was a strange one—a kind of aimless anger directed at something he couldn't identify. Even two weeks later, he remembered exactly how he had felt. He had been puzzled by the intensity of his irritation and had never once thought to connect his bad mood to the encounter that morning. Still, he had been in a foul temper all day.

The man with the crape band didn't take long to remind Velchaninoff of his presence. The very next day, they crossed paths again, this time on the Nefsky Prospect, and once again, the man stared at him with that same fixed, peculiar look.

Velchaninoff became furious, spitting on the ground in irritation—a very Russian reaction. But just a moment later, he found himself wondering why he had been so angry. "There are some faces," he thought, "that you dislike at first sight for no reason. But I've definitely seen that man somewhere before."

"Yes, I've seen him before," he muttered to himself half an hour later.

As on the first occasion, Velchaninoff remained in a terrible mood for the rest of the evening. That night, he even had a bad dream. Still, it never occurred to him that his sour temper might have been caused by running into the man in mourning. Even though he recalled and thought about the encounter two or three times that evening, the connection never crossed his mind.

He grew angry at himself for letting "such a shabby-looking fellow" linger in his thoughts. The very idea that someone so insignificant could affect his mood seemed humiliating to him.

Two days later, they met yet again, this time at the landing of one of the small Neva ferry steamers.

On this third occasion, Velchaninoff was convinced the man recognized him. He seemed to push through the crowd, heading directly toward Velchaninoff, and might have even stretched out his hand and called him by name. Though, about the last detail, Velchaninoff wasn't entirely sure. "Who on earth is he?" Velchaninoff wondered. "And if he does recognize me and wants to talk, why doesn't he just come up and speak instead of acting like this?"

With these thoughts running through his mind, Velchaninoff climbed into a droshky and headed to the Smolney Monastery, where his lawyer lived.

Half an hour later, he was locked in one of his usual arguments with the lawyer.

That evening, Velchaninoff's mood was worse than ever, and his night was filled with unpleasant dreams and wild imaginings. The next morning, as he looked at himself in the mirror, he muttered, "It must be my liver."

That was the third time they had met.

For five days, there was no sign of the man. Yet, much to his annoyance, Velchaninoff couldn't stop thinking about the man with the crape band.

He caught himself wondering about him. "What does he have to do with me?" he thought. "What could his business in St. Petersburg be? He looks busy enough. And who is he mourning? He clearly knows me, but I have no idea who he is! And why do people like him even wear crape bands on their hats? It just doesn't seem to fit someone like that. I think I'd recognize him if I could get a proper look at him."

He was gripped by a feeling many of us know well—the same frustration as when you can't remember a specific word. All the related words come to mind, and you recall times you've used the word, but the actual word itself just won't surface, no matter how hard you try.

"Let's see," he mused. "It was... yes... some time ago. It was... where exactly? There was a... oh, to hell with it! What does it matter to me anyway?" He broke off angrily. "I'm not going to lower myself by thinking about some insignificant nobody like him!"

He felt furious. But later that evening, when he remembered how upset he had been and recalled the cause of his anger, he felt a sharp, uncomfortable sense of shame, as if he had been caught doing something wrong.

This realization unsettled and irritated him.

"There has to be some reason why I get so angry just from remembering that man's face," he thought, though he didn't finish the thought.

The next evening, he found himself even angrier—and this time, he felt he had a good reason. "Such nerve is unbelievable!" he said to himself.

The truth was, there had been a fourth encounter with the man in the crape-banded hat. It was as if the man had appeared out of nowhere to confront him. Here's what happened:

Velchaninoff had just accidentally run into the state councillor he had been so eager to see. He had been planning to catch the councillor by surprise at his country house, but now their meeting had happened by chance. The councillor clearly wanted to avoid Velchaninoff, but Velchaninoff needed him badly for his lawsuit. When they met, Velchaninoff was delighted, while the councillor was anything but.

Velchaninoff quickly grabbed his arm and walked alongside him, determined to get the information he needed. He worked hard to steer the conversation toward the important topic, all while the sly councillor did his best to say as little as possible. At that crucial moment, when Velchaninoff's full attention was focused on catching any useful hint from his companion, he glanced away for just an instant—and there, across the street, was the man with the crape band. He was walking along, watching Velchaninoff intently. Not only that, but he seemed to be smiling!

"Damn him!" Velchaninoff exploded in a fit of rage, while the "old fox" quickly disappeared. "I would have succeeded in another minute! Curse that filthy little pest! He's just spying on me. I'll—I'll hire someone to deal with him. I swear he laughed at me! Damn him, I'll beat him. If only I had a stick right now—I'll buy one! I'm not letting this go. Who is he? I'll find out! Who is he?"

Three days after this fourth encounter, Velchaninoff was sitting down to dinner at his usual restaurant, in a mood that bordered on fury. No matter how much pride he had, he couldn't deny to himself that his irritation, anxiety, and overall agitation were undeniably linked to that shabby-looking man with the crape band.

"Maybe I'm just a hypochondriac," he thought, "and maybe I'm making a mountain out of a molehill. But what good does it do me to believe it's all in my head? If every little wretch like that can throw me into such turmoil, then—it's—well, it's simply unbearable!"

At today's fifth meeting, the "elephant" had indeed proven to be a mere "gnat." The man with the crape band had appeared as suddenly as ever but passed Velchaninoff without even looking at him. In fact, he kept his eyes down and seemed to be trying not to attract any attention. Velchaninoff spun around and shouted at him as loudly as he could.

"Hey!" he yelled. "You! Crape band! Trying to go unnoticed this time, are you? Who are you?"

Both the question and the act of yelling after the man were absurdly foolish, and Velchaninoff knew it the moment he spoke. The man turned around, paused for a moment, seemed confused, and gave an awkward smile. He looked as if he was about to say something but hesitated, standing there in visible indecision for half a minute. Then, without a word, he turned sharply and hurried away. Velchaninoff stared after him, amazed. "What if I'm haunting him instead of him haunting me?" he thought.

Nevertheless, Velchaninoff finished his dinner and then decided to visit the state councillor's house unannounced. Upon arriving, he learned the councillor wasn't home and likely wouldn't return until three or four in the morning, as he was attending a name-day party.

Furious, Velchaninoff decided to hunt the man down at the party. He even climbed into a droshky with the wild idea of barging into the celebration. Luckily, he reconsidered on the way, got out of the vehicle, and walked toward the Great Theatre near his home instead. He felt a strong need to move and knew he absolutely had to get a good night's sleep. To ensure he would be tired enough to rest, he walked all the way home—a long walk that left him exhausted by the time he arrived at half-past ten.

His lodgings, which he had rented in March and had been complaining about ever since, were not nearly as bad as he liked to claim. He often excused his living situation by reminding himself it was only temporary and that he had ended up in St. Petersburg purely by accident because of that cursed lawsuit.

The entrance to the building was indeed a bit dark and dingy, located under the archway of the gateway. However, Velchaninoff had two large, bright rooms on the second floor, separated by an entrance hall. One room faced the yard, while the other overlooked the street. Off the room facing the yard was a smaller bedroom, but Velchaninoff had crammed it with piles of books and papers. He preferred to sleep in the larger room overlooking the street.

His bed was set up daily on the large divan. The rooms were furnished with good pieces, and a few valuable ornaments and paintings were scattered about, but the entire place was in a state of chaos. At the time, Velchaninoff had no regular servant. His one housekeeper had left to visit her friends in the countryside. He had considered hiring a manservant but decided it wasn't worth the trouble for such a short time. Besides, he disliked servants. Instead, he made arrangements with Martha, the dvornik's sister, to come in every morning and tidy up his rooms. He would leave her the key when he went out for the day. However, Martha did almost nothing to clean the place and even stole from him, but Velchaninoff didn't mind. He enjoyed having the house to himself. Solitude, though, has its limits, and Velchaninoff found his nerves couldn't handle the loneliness during his darker moods. Over time, he began to loathe his rooms more and more every time he stepped inside.

On this particular evening, however, he barely gave himself time to undress. He threw himself onto the bed, determined not to think about anything, and willed himself to fall asleep immediately.

Strangely enough, as soon as his head hit the pillow, he actually drifted off. This was the first time in a month he had managed to fall asleep so quickly.

He woke up around two in the morning, feeling deeply unsettled. He had been dreaming strange, fragmented dreams that reminded him of the feverish ramblings of someone ill.

The dream centered on a crime he had committed and hidden but for which he was now being accused by a never-ending stream of people pouring into his rooms. The crowd inside was already enormous, yet more people kept arriving, and the door never stayed shut.

What drew all his attention, however, was one peculiar man. This figure seemed to have been someone very close to him in the past, someone deeply connected to him. The man had been dead for some time but now reappeared for reasons unknown.

The most tormenting part was that Velchaninoff couldn't remember who the man was. He couldn't even recall his name, though he vaguely remembered loving him once. Everyone in the room seemed to be waiting for this man to speak, as if his words alone would either condemn or justify Velchaninoff. The crowd grew restless in their anticipation, eager to hear him say something.

But the man sat silently at the table, refusing to utter a single word.

The noise in the room grew louder, the frustration escalated, and finally, in a fit of rage, Velchaninoff stormed up to the man and struck him for his silence. Oddly, he felt a twisted satisfaction in hitting him, even as his heart froze with horror at what he had done. The sensation of guilt and the satisfaction from his action seemed intertwined.

Driven by growing anger and despair, he struck the man again and then a third time. Soon, in a frenzy of fear and madness—a state of mind so intense it bordered on insanity, yet somehow carried an element of cruel satisfaction—Velchaninoff lost count of the blows. He struck again and again, relentless in his fury.

He felt an overwhelming urge to destroy, to obliterate, to erase everything in front of him.

Suddenly, something extraordinary happened. The crowd erupted in a collective, terrible cry and turned to face the door. At the same moment, the hall bell rang three times, each peal so loud and forceful it seemed as though someone was trying to rip the bell out of its place.

Velchaninoff woke with a start, instantly leaping to his feet. He rushed to the door, convinced that the ringing had been real, not a part of his dream. Someone had rung the bell, and they were standing at his front door right now.

It seemed too strange that such a loud, clear ring could be part of a dream, Velchaninoff thought. But, to his surprise, that turned out to be exactly the case. He opened the door and stepped out onto the landing. He looked down the stairs and around, but no one was there. The bell hung motionless. Surprised but relieved, he returned to his room. Lighting a candle, he suddenly remembered that he had left the door closed but not locked or chained. This wasn't unusual for him; on other nights, he had come home and forgotten to lock the door, though his maid had often scolded him for it when she was there. Now, he went back to the hall to secure the door. Before doing so, he opened it one more time and glanced around the staircase. Then he shut the door, fastened the chain and hook, but didn't bother turning the key in the lock.

At that moment, a clock struck half-past two. He realized he had slept for about three hours.

The dream had unsettled him so much that he didn't want to lie back down immediately. Instead, he decided to pace the room for a while and smoke a cigar. Half-dressed, he went to the window, pulled aside the thick curtains, and raised one of the blinds. It was already nearly full daylight. The bright summer nights of St. Petersburg always bothered his nerves, and lately, they had made his sleeplessness worse. A few weeks earlier, he had bought heavy curtains to block the light completely when drawn.

Now, as the sunlight poured in, he ignored the lit candle on the table and began pacing the room. The dream still weighed on his mind, leaving behind a lingering guilt. He couldn't shake the awful feeling from having struck "that man" in the dream. "But it wasn't real!" he argued with himself. "It was just a dream! Why get upset over something that didn't happen?"

Velchaninoff became increasingly convinced that he was unwell, that his physical health was affecting his mental state. He thought of himself as an invalid.

He had always hated the idea of growing old or weak, though in his angrier moments, he liked to exaggerate these fears to torment himself further.

"It's old age," he muttered as he paced. "I'm turning into an old fool, that's what it is! I'm losing my memory—seeing ghosts, dreaming nonsense, hearing bells that aren't ringing. Damn it all! I've had dreams like this before, and they always mean I'm coming down with a fever. Maybe this whole thing with the man and the crape hatband is a dream too! I was right yesterday—it's not him haunting me, I'm the one haunting him! I've made up a ghost story about him and now I'm scared of my own imagination! And why do I call him a little cad? For all I know, he might be a perfectly respectable man! His face is unpleasant, sure, but it's not monstrous. He dresses like anyone else. I don't know, there's just something about his look... There I go again! What does it matter what his look is? What an idiot I am, acting like I can't live without obsessing over this wretched man. Damn him!"

One thought about the man particularly troubled Velchaninoff. He was certain he had known this person before, and not just in passing— they had been close. Now, whenever they met, Velchaninoff felt like the man was laughing at him, either because he knew some deep secret about Velchaninoff's past or because he enjoyed seeing him in his current state of humiliation and poverty.

Velchaninoff instinctively walked to the window for some fresh air but stopped abruptly, seized by a shiver. He suddenly felt that something strange and extraordinary was happening right in front of him.

Before he could open the window, something outside made him step back behind the curtain and hide.

The man with the crape hatband was standing on the opposite side of the street.

He stood there facing Velchaninoff's window, though it seemed he didn't know Velchaninoff was watching him. The man appeared to be studying the house carefully, as if considering some question about it.

After a moment, he seemed to reach a decision. He tapped his forehead with his finger, glanced around calmly, and then darted across the street on tiptoe. He entered the gate, which was often left open during summer nights until two or three in the morning.

"He's coming to me," Velchaninoff muttered. With the same cautious movements, he left the window and hurried to the front door. Standing in the hallway, he placed his trembling hand on the hook he had secured just a few minutes earlier and waited, holding his breath. He strained to hear the sound of footsteps approaching the stairs, but his own racing heartbeat was so loud he feared it might drown out the noise.

He couldn't make sense of what was happening, but it felt as if his dream was coming true.

Velchaninoff was naturally courageous, often drawn to risky situations just for the thrill, even when there was no one around to witness his daring. But this felt different. He wasn't quite himself, though his bravery remained intact—only now, it was charged with something new and intense. He listened closely, tracking the stranger's movements from behind the door.

"Ah, there he is—on the steps now! He's coming up! Now he's looking around, crouching down. Aha! His hand is on the door handle—he's trying it! He thought it would be unlocked. Then he must know I sometimes forget to lock it! He's trying again—maybe he thinks the hook might slip. He doesn't want to leave without doing something!"

Velchaninoff's thoughts mirrored the man's actions perfectly. There was no mistaking it—someone was outside, gently testing the door handle, tugging the door cautiously, clearly attempting to enter. It was just as clear that whoever was outside had a purpose for sneaking into another person's home in the dead of night. But Velchaninoff had already decided on his plan. He would wait for the right moment, unhook the door, fling it wide open, and confront this mysterious figure face-to-face to demand an explanation.

The plan was set, and now it was time to act.

When the moment felt right, Velchaninoff swiftly unhooked the door, threw it open, and nearly stumbled straight into the man with the crape hatband!

Chapter 3

The man with the crape hatband froze in place, completely stunned.

Both men stood on the landing, staring directly into each other's eyes, silent and unmoving.

Several moments passed, and suddenly, like a bolt of lightning, Velchaninoff realized who his unexpected visitor was.

At the same time, the visitor seemed to recognize that Velchaninoff had identified him. Velchaninoff saw it in his expression. In an instant, the man's entire face lit up with the sweetest smile, an expression so out of place it seemed almost absurd.

"Surely, I have the pleasure of addressing Aleksey Ivanovitch?" the man asked in a soft, almost syrupy voice, completely at odds with the situation.

"And you must be Pavel Pavlovitch Trusotsky?" Velchaninoff replied after a pause, his face full of confusion.

"I had the pleasure of your acquaintance ten years ago in T——, and, if you'll recall, we were almost close friends," said the visitor.

"Yes, yes, that's true," Velchaninoff replied. "But it's three o'clock in the morning, and you've been fiddling with my lock for the last ten minutes."

"Three o'clock!" Pavel Pavlovitch exclaimed, checking his watch with a look of regretful surprise.

"So it is! My goodness—three o'clock! Please forgive me, Aleksey Ivanovitch. I should have realized the time before deciding to visit. I'll take my leave now and explain another time."

"Oh no—no, no! If you're going to explain, do it now, right here and now," Velchaninoff interrupted, his voice heated. "Please step inside! You must have meant to come in; you didn't just come all this way in the middle of the night to play with my lock for fun."

He felt agitated but also oddly uneasy. His thoughts were scattered, and he was frustrated with himself for it. There was no real danger, no mystery—just Pavel Pavlovitch, standing there awkwardly.

Yet, despite himself, Velchaninoff couldn't shake the sense that something was off. A shadow of unease lingered, an apprehension about something unknown.

He gestured for Pavel Pavlovitch to come in, guided him to a chair, and then sat on the edge of his bed a few feet away. Resting his elbows on his knees, Velchaninoff stared at his visitor, waiting for him to speak.

But strangely, Pavel Pavlovitch remained silent. He didn't seem to realize it was his turn to explain. Instead, he sat there, staring back at Velchaninoff with an expectant look, as if waiting for him to speak first. Maybe he felt a little uneasy at first, like a mouse caught in a trap.

Velchaninoff quickly lost his patience.

"Well?" he demanded. "You're not a ghost or some kind of illusion, are you? You're not dead, right? Come on, man, this isn't a joke. I need an explanation!"

The visitor shifted in his seat, gave a nervous smile, and started to speak cautiously.

"If I understand correctly," he said, "what surprises you is the time of my visit and the way I came here. Honestly, when I think about our past and how close we were, I'm surprised at myself too. But the truth is, I didn't even mean to come inside. It just happened."

"Just happened? I saw you sneaking across the road on tiptoes!"

"You saw me? Well then, you probably know as much about this as I do, maybe even more. But I see that I'm bothering you. Here's the situation: I've been in town for about three weeks on business. My name is Pavel Pavlovitch Trusotsky, as you already recognized. I'm here trying to transfer to a new department—a position with a much better salary. But none of that really matters. The truth is, I think I've been stalling. Even if everything was settled right now, I'd probably still be hanging around in your St. Petersburg in my current state of mind. I've been wandering around aimlessly, as though I've lost interest in everything—and, in a strange way, I don't even mind it."

"What state of mind?" Velchaninoff asked, frowning.

The visitor looked up at Velchaninoff, picked up his hat from the floor, and, with a dramatic air, pointed to the black crape band around it.

"There, sir. That's the state of mind," he said.

Velchaninoff stared blankly at the crape, then back at the man's face. Suddenly, a flush of heat rose to his cheeks, and he became visibly agitated.

"Not Natalia Vasilievna?" he asked, almost in disbelief.

"Yes, Natalia Vasilievna," the man replied. "She passed last March. Consumption—it happened so quickly. Just two or three months, and then it was all over. And now, here I am, as you see me."

With that, Pavel Pavlovitch bowed his bald head, holding it down for several seconds. In one hand, he held his hat with its mourning band, as though it explained everything. The gesture and his demeanor were full of exaggerated emotion.

This display seemed to bring a faint, sarcastic smile to Velchaninoff's face. It lasted only a moment, though, because the news of Natalia Vasilievna's death—someone he had known so long ago and forgotten for many years—had unexpectedly shaken him.

"Unbelievable," he murmured, saying the first thing that came to mind. "Why didn't you come and tell me sooner?"

"Thank you for your concern," Pavel Pavlovitch replied. "I see and appreciate it, despite—"

"Despite what?" Velchaninoff interrupted.

"In spite of so many years apart, you immediately shared in my grief—and even in me, personally—so fully that I feel naturally grateful to you. That's all I wanted to say, sir! Don't think I'm doubting my friends; even here, I can point out several very genuine ones (for example, Stepan Michailovitch Bagantoff). But remember, dear Aleksey Ivanovitch, it's been nine years since we were acquainted—or friends, if you'll allow me to call it that—and in all that time, you never visited us, never wrote."

Pavel Pavlovitch said all this in a singsong tone, as if he were reciting from a script, but kept his eyes downcast, though he clearly saw everything happening above his lowered lashes.

By this time, Velchaninoff had collected his thoughts.

With an odd, growing fascination, he kept staring at Pavel Pavlovitch, listening intently. Suddenly, when the latter stopped speaking, a wave of curious thoughts swept unexpectedly through Velchaninoff's mind.

"But wait," he exclaimed. "How did I not recognize you before now? We've met at least five times on the street!"

"That's true—I'm fully aware of that. You happened to see me two or three times, and—"

"No, no! You ran into me, not the other way around!" Velchaninoff suddenly burst into laughter and stood up. Pavel Pavlovitch hesitated for a moment, gave him a sharp look, then continued.

"As for you not recognizing me, it's understandable. First, you might have forgotten me by now. Also, I've had smallpox since we last met, and I imagine it's left some marks on my face."

"Smallpox? How on earth did that happen?—But yes, you've had it, no doubt about that!" Velchaninoff laughed again. "What a peculiar fellow you are! Well, go on, don't stop."

Velchaninoff's mood was steadily lifting. That earlier agitation, which had unsettled him so much, had given way to a strange lightheartedness. He began pacing back and forth across the room with quick steps.

"I was saying," Pavel Pavlovitch continued, "that even though I've seen you a few times, and planned to visit you when I came to Petersburg, I was in such a state of mind, you know, and my wits have been so scrambled since last March, that—"

"Your wits? Since last March? Go on—hold on a second. Do you smoke?"

"Oh, you know, Natalia Vasilievna never—"

"Of course. But since March?"

"Well, maybe just a cigarette now and then."

"Here, take one! Light it and continue—you're fascinating me."

Velchaninoff lit a cigar and sat back down on the edge of his bed. Pavel Pavlovitch paused for a moment.

"But you seem quite agitated yourself," Pavel Pavlovitch observed. "Are you feeling all right?"

"Oh, to hell with my health!" Velchaninoff snapped. "Just keep going!"

Pavel Pavlovitch noticed his host's agitation and seemed pleased by it. With growing confidence, he carried on with his story.

"What should I talk about?" he asked. "Imagine me, Alexey Ivanovitch—a man completely broken—not just broken, but destroyed at the very core. After twenty years of marriage, I'm left to wander aimlessly along dusty roads, my mind scattered, almost forgetting who I am, and yet somehow finding a strange, almost intoxicating pleasure in my solitude. Isn't it natural that in such a moment of forgetting myself, I might stumble upon an old friend—a dear friend—and feel like avoiding him? And isn't it just as natural that in another moment, I might desperately want to see someone who was a witness to, or even a part of, my past—my unforgettable past? To rush to them—not just during the day, but even in the dead of night if needed—to embrace them, even if it means waking them at three in the morning! I might have been wrong about the timing, but not about my choice of friend. Right now, I feel the full joy of success. My reckless decision worked—I've found understanding! As for the late hour, I honestly thought it wasn't even midnight yet. You see, grief does something to you—it intoxicates you. Or maybe it's not grief exactly—it's this new state of mind I'm in that overwhelms me."

"Goodness, the way you talk is so strange!" Velchaninoff said, standing up again and becoming more serious.

"Is it strange? Maybe."

"Tell me, are you joking?"

"Joking?" Pavel Pavlovitch exclaimed, sounding deeply offended. "Joking—when I'm speaking about—"

"Oh, stop that! For heaven's sake, enough of that."

Velchaninoff resumed pacing up and down the room.

For about five minutes, neither of them said anything. Pavel Pavlovitch seemed as though he might get up from his chair, but Velchaninoff motioned for him to stay seated, and Pavel Pavlovitch obediently sank back into his chair.

"How different you've become!" Velchaninoff finally said, stopping in front of him as if struck by a sudden realization. "So utterly different!"

"Really! Am I that different?" Pavel Pavlovitch asked.

"It's astonishing! You're a completely different person!"

"Well, it's not surprising—nine years, after all!"

"No, no, no! It's not just the years! This isn't about how you look—it's something else."

"Well, nine years could explain anything," Pavel Pavlovitch said.

"Or maybe it's only since March?" Velchaninoff added.

"Ha-ha! You're teasing me," Pavel Pavlovitch replied, chuckling slyly. "But, if I may ask, what exactly is it that makes me seem so changed?"

"Oh—why, you used to be such a steady, serious, and proper Pavel Pavlovitch. So wise and respectable. Now, you're just a useless sort of Pavel Pavlovitch."

Velchaninoff was in that kind of irritated mood where even the calmest person might say more than they intend.

"Useless, am I? And not wise anymore, huh?" Pavel Pavlovitch chuckled with an unpleasant satisfaction.

"Wise? My dear sir, I'm afraid you're not even sober," Velchaninoff replied sharply, adding to himself, "I may be pretty rude, but I've got nothing on this little scoundrel! And what in the world is he trying to get at?"

"Oh, my dear, good, best Alexey Ivanovitch," Pavel Pavlovitch suddenly exclaimed, twisting nervously in his chair, "why should I be sober? We're not strolling through the bright circles of high society, you and I, at the moment. We're just two old friends, reunited in the purest spirit of affection, to remember and talk about the cherished bond we shared—the one that dear departed soul so beautifully embodied in our friendship."

As he said this, the emotional Pavel Pavlovitch got so swept up in his feelings that he lowered his head again, this time burying his face in his hat to hide his supposed emotion.

Velchaninoff watched him, feeling a growing sense of discomfort and disgust.

"I can't help but think he's just plain stupid," Velchaninoff thought. "But no, no—his face is so flushed, he must be drunk. Drunk or not, though, what does this little creep want from me? That's the real question."

"Do you remember—oh, don't you remember—those wonderful evenings? Sometimes dancing, sometimes reading—at Simeon Simeonovitch's?" Pavel Pavlovitch continued, slowly lowering the hat from his face and becoming more enthusiastic as he reminisced. "And our little readings—you, me, and her. And the first time we met! You came in asking for information about your business in town, yelling at me right away—don't you remember? Then, suddenly, Natalia Vasilievna walked in, and within ten minutes, you were our dear friend. You stayed that way for exactly a year! Just like Turgeniev's story, The Provincial Lady!"

Velchaninoff paced up and down the room as the tirade went on, his eyes fixed on the floor. He listened impatiently, disgusted, but he still couldn't help listening closely.

"It never occurred to me to think about The Provincial Lady in connection with all that," Velchaninoff interrupted. "And listen—why are you talking in that sniveling, wheedling voice? You never used to talk like this. Your whole behavior is so unlike you."

"Quite right, quite right. I used to be more reserved, I know. I preferred listening while others spoke. Do you remember how wonderfully the dear departed used to talk? Her wit, her charm. As for The Provincial Lady, she and I often compared your friendship with us to certain parts of that story, especially to what one Stupendiev does. It was remarkably similar to his character and actions."

"What Stupendief are you talking about, for heaven's sake?" Velchaninoff shouted, stomping his foot in frustration. The name seemed to stir up some deeply irritating thoughts in his mind.

"Why, Stupendief, don't you know? The 'husband' in The Provincial Lady," Pavel Pavlovitch said in the sweetest tone, practically whining. "But that's from a different set of fond memories—after you left, actually, when Mr. Bagantoff honored us with his friendship, just like you had before him, only his lasted five whole years."

"Bagantoff? Which Bagantoff? You mean the same Bagantoff who was working in your town? Why, he also—"

"Yes, yes! Exactly! He also!" Pavel Pavlovitch exclaimed, latching onto Velchaninoff's accidental slip. "Of course! So there you have it—the whole cast. Bagantoff was the 'count,' the dear departed was the 'Provincial Lady,' and I was the 'husband,' though I suppose I was removed from the role for incompetence!"

"Yes, I can't imagine you as Stupendief. You're—well, you're Pavel Pavlovitch Trusotsky, first and foremost," Velchaninoff replied scornfully. "But look here! Bagantoff is in town. I've seen him myself. Why don't you go see him instead of bothering me?"

"My dear sir, I've been going there every day for three weeks. He won't see me. He's ill and can't receive visitors! And, you know, I've discovered he truly is very ill! Imagine my feelings—a five-year friendship! Oh, my dear Alexey Ivanovitch! You can't understand what I'm feeling in my current state of mind. One moment, I wish the earth would swallow me whole; the next, I'm desperate to find an old friend, a witness to the past, just to cry on his shoulder—just to cry, I swear."

"Well, don't you think that's enough for tonight?" Velchaninoff cut in sharply.

"Oh, far too much!" Pavel Pavlovitch replied, standing up. "It must be four o'clock already, and here I am, troubling you with my selfish rambling."

"Now, listen. I'll come to see you myself tomorrow, and then maybe—wait, be honest. Are you drunk right now?"

"Drunk? Not in the least!"

"Did you drink anything before you came here—or earlier in the day?"

"My dear Alexey Ivanovitch, you're burning up with a fever, I swear!"

"Goodnight. I'll come tomorrow."

"And I noticed it all evening—really, you're quite delirious!" Pavel Pavlovitch added, almost savoring the moment. "I feel terrible for having upset you so clumsily. Well, well, I'll leave now. You must lie down immediately and get some rest."

"You haven't told me where you're staying," Velchaninoff shouted after him as he left.

"Oh, didn't I? The Pokrofsky Hotel."

Pavel Pavlovitch was already on the stairs.

"Wait!" Velchaninoff called out again. "You're not running away, are you?"

"What do you mean by 'running away'?" Pavel Pavlovitch asked, turning back on the third step with an exaggerated grin and wide-open eyes.

Instead of answering, Velchaninoff slammed the door shut with all his might, locked and bolted it, and stormed back into his room. Once inside, he spat on the ground as though to rid himself of a bad taste.

He stood still in the middle of the room for at least five minutes before finally throwing himself onto his bed and falling asleep instantly.

The forgotten candle burned itself out in its holder.

Chapter 4

Velchaninoff slept deeply until half-past nine. At that time, he suddenly woke up, sat on the edge of his bed, and began to think. His thoughts quickly settled on the news of "that woman's" death.

The shock from hearing about her passing the previous day had left him feeling disturbed and unsettled. Now, all the events from nine years ago came flooding back with remarkable clarity.

He had loved this woman, Natalia Vasilievna—Trusotsky's wife. He had loved her and played the role of her lover during the time he stayed in her provincial town while handling some business related to a legacy. Although his work didn't require him to stay there for so long, he ended up living there for an entire year, held back by his involvement with her.

His feelings for Natalia Vasilievna had completely overwhelmed him, making him her willing servant. At the time, he would have done anything, no matter how trivial or unreasonable, to please her. Never before or since had he felt anything close to the obsession she inspired in him.

When it was finally time for him to leave, Velchaninoff was so devastated, even though the separation was supposed to be brief, that he begged Natalia Vasilievna to leave everything behind and flee across the border with him. At first, she seemed to entertain the idea, likely as a joke, but then she laughed at him and mocked his suggestion until he reluctantly agreed to leave on his own.

Yet, within two months of arriving in St. Petersburg, he began to ask himself a question that he had never been able to answer: "Did I truly love her, or was it just an infatuation?" It wasn't as though he had fallen in love with someone else. In fact, during those first two months, he had been so emotionally drained that he hadn't even looked at another woman, despite returning to his usual social routines. Still, he knew with certainty that if he were to return to her town, he would immediately fall back under her spell, even though he still couldn't decide whether his feelings for her were genuine love or just a fleeting obsession.

Five years later, he felt just as sure of this, though by then the thought of her filled him with disgust. Even hearing her name made him feel ashamed and bitter. He couldn't understand how he had ever allowed himself to be consumed by such a foolish passion. Thinking about it made him blush with embarrassment, and he had even shed tears of shame over it.

Over time, he managed to suppress his feelings of regret and convinced himself that he had moved on. But now, nine years later, the news of Natalia's death had brought everything back to the surface.

As Velchaninoff sat on his bed, his thoughts racing, he found some consolation in knowing that she was gone, even though her name still stirred painful memories.

"Surely I feel a little sorry for her?" he wondered.

At least he no longer felt the same hatred he once did. Now, he could think about her without any strong emotions clouding his judgment, allowing him to reflect on her more fairly.

Velchaninoff had long believed that Natalia Vasilievna was likely no different from any other woman in good provincial society and that he had imagined much of her charm and allure. However, despite this conclusion, he often doubted its accuracy. There were facts that contradicted his theory. For example, Bagantoff, who had spent several years in T——, was just as captivated by her as Velchaninoff had been, unable to resist her influence. Bagantoff, though young and, as

Velchaninoff called him, "an idiot," was from one of the most prestigious families in St. Petersburg. His career and future were tied to that city, yet he had wasted five crucial years of his life in T——, solely because of his love for Natalia Vasilievna. It was even said that he only left for St. Petersburg after she grew tired of him. All of this suggested that there was something uniquely compelling about Natalia Vasilievna.

Yet Natalia was neither wealthy nor beautiful. In fact, she might have been considered plain. Velchaninoff had known her when she was twenty-eight. While her face could sometimes adopt a pleasant expression, her eyes were too cold and hard. She was thin and bony in appearance. Although intelligent, her mind was narrow and biased. She had impeccable taste, particularly in clothing, and her character was strong and domineering. She was never wrong in her own eyes, nor did she ever feel remorse for being unfaithful to her husband. She despised corruption yet was corrupt herself. Velchaninoff believed she was completely convinced of her own moral integrity. He thought she truly didn't realize that her behavior was immoral. To him, she was one of those women who seemed destined to be unfaithful wives. Such women, in his view, always married because it was in their nature. Their first lover was always their husband, and if they were later unfaithful, they always considered the husband at fault while seeing themselves as entirely blameless and innocent.

This was how Velchaninoff saw Natalia, and he was sure such a type of woman existed. He was equally convinced there was a corresponding type of man, specifically suited to be the husbands of such women. These men, in his opinion, were destined to be "permanent husbands," existing solely for the role of being a husband and nothing more.

Velchaninoff had no doubt about these two archetypes, and he considered Pavel Pavlovitch Trusotsky a prime example of the male

41

type. However, the Pavel Pavlovitch he met last night was very different from the one he had known in T——. Upon reflection, Velchaninoff realized that the change was to be expected. Pavel Pavlovitch could only remain the man he had been as long as his wife was alive. Now, he seemed incomplete, like a fragment of something larger, left to wander aimlessly—a strange and unbalanced being.

As for the Pavel Pavlovitch of T——, Velchaninoff remembered him clearly. Pavel Pavlovitch had been a husband, first and foremost. That was his primary role, and everything else he did was secondary to it. Even his work as a department clerk seemed to be done in service to his responsibilities as a husband, contributing to his wife's status and social position. At the time, he was thirty-five years old, owned a fair amount of property, and held a respectable position. While he displayed no exceptional talent, he was also not incompetent. His career and reputation were solid, reflecting his role as a dutiful, if unremarkable, husband.

Natalia Vasilievna was respected and admired by everyone around her, though she didn't care about their admiration—she simply saw it as something she deserved. She was an excellent hostess and had trained Pavel Pavlovitch to be polite enough to host and entertain the best society with decent manners.

Whether Pavel Pavlovitch was intelligent or not, Velchaninoff couldn't say, since Natalia Vasilievna preferred him to speak as little as possible, leaving little chance to assess his mind. He might have had both good and bad qualities, but the good ones seemed locked away, while the bad ones were carefully suppressed. Velchaninoff remembered that Pavel Pavlovitch had, on occasion, tried to poke fun at others, but this behavior was quickly stopped. He had once enjoyed telling stories, but even that habit was strictly regulated—only short, dull anecdotes were allowed.

Pavel Pavlovitch also had a group of friends outside their home with whom he would sometimes drink, but Natalia Vasilievna swiftly put an end to this "bad habit."

Despite all this, Natalia Vasilievna appeared, to outsiders, to be the most submissive and devoted wife. She likely thought of herself that way too. As for whether Pavel Pavlovitch truly loved her, no one could say.

While living in T——, Velchaninoff often wondered if Pavel Pavlovitch ever suspected the affair between his wife and himself. He had repeatedly asked Natalia Vasilievna if her husband knew about their relationship, but she would always answer with some irritation that Pavel Pavlovitch neither knew nor ever would know. "And even if he did," she would add, "it's none of his business!"

Another unusual trait of Natalia Vasilievna was that she never mocked Pavel Pavlovitch and never treated him as a joke. She would immediately defend him against anyone who dared to disrespect him.

Pavel Pavlovitch's nostalgic mention of the trio's readings from nine years ago was accurate. They used to read Dickens' novels together, with either Velchaninoff or Pavel Pavlovitch reading aloud while Natalia Vasilievna worked. Velchaninoff's life in T—— came to an abrupt and deeply painful end. Essentially, he was discarded, though the whole process was so skillfully managed that he didn't even realize what was happening until it was too late.

A month before Velchaninoff left, a young artillery officer had come to town and befriended the Trusotskys. The group of three soon became four. Shortly after, Natalia Vasilievna insisted that Velchaninoff needed to leave. She offered countless reasons why his departure was necessary, and one argument, in particular, seemed to settle the matter. Velchaninoff's attempt to persuade her to run away with him—to Paris or anywhere—ended in failure. He finally left for

St. Petersburg, reluctantly agreeing to a two- or three-month absence, and only because she convinced him that it was for the best.

Two months later, he received a letter from Natalia Vasilievna. She begged him not to return to T——, confessing that she had fallen in love with someone else. The reason she had initially given for his departure, she admitted, had been a mistake. Velchaninoff thought of the young officer and understood. That was the end of their affair.

A year or two after this, Bagantoff appeared in T—— and developed a close relationship with Natalia Vasilievna that lasted five years. Velchaninoff attributed this unusual stretch of fidelity to Natalia's advancing age.

Sitting on his bed for almost an hour, Velchaninoff replayed these memories in his mind. Finally, he snapped out of his thoughts, rang for Mavra to bring his coffee, drank it quickly, and dressed. By eleven o'clock, he was on his way to the Pokrofsky Hotel. He felt somewhat embarrassed about how he had treated Pavel Pavlovitch the night before. Velchaninoff chalked up the bizarre events—the lock, the strange behavior—to Pavel Pavlovitch being drunk and other unimportant reasons. Still, he couldn't quite explain why he was now heading to see the husband of a woman with whom his ties had ended so naturally and conclusively. Yet, an irresistible force seemed to draw him there, and he followed it.

Chapter 5

Pavel Pavlovitch wasn't thinking of "running away," and even Velchaninoff himself couldn't explain why he had asked him that question last night. It made no sense.

Following the directions he was given, Velchaninoff arrived at the Petrofsky Hotel and quickly found the place. He was informed that Pavel Pavlovitch had moved into a furnished apartment in the back part of the same building.

As he climbed the narrow, dirty staircase to the third floor, he suddenly heard crying. It sounded like a young child, about seven or eight years old. The crying was bitter but muffled, as though the child was trying not to be too loud. At the same time, a man's voice could be heard trying to quiet the child, but instead of comforting, the voice only seemed to make the sobbing worse. The child seemed to be begging for forgiveness, and the man's tone lacked any real sympathy.

Reaching a dimly lit hallway with doors on either side, Velchaninoff came across a stout, older woman dressed sloppily in morning attire. He asked her where Pavel Pavlovitch was.

She pointed to one of the doors, the same one where the sounds were coming from. Her plump face flushed with what seemed like indignation as she tapped on it with her fingers.

"It sounds like he's having fun in there!" she said, and then headed down the stairs.

Velchaninoff raised his hand to knock but thought better of it. Instead, he opened the door without hesitation.

In the middle of a modestly furnished yet cluttered room stood Pavel Pavlovitch, red-faced and in his shirt sleeves. He was trying to get a little girl to do something, using a mix of shouts, gestures, and what looked to Velchaninoff like the threat of kicks to get his way. The girl, around seven or eight years old, was poorly dressed in a short black dress. She was hysterical, crying loudly, and stretching her arms toward Pavel Pavlovitch as if pleading with him to let her do something she desperately wanted.

The moment Velchaninoff entered the room, everything changed. The girl, upon seeing him, let out a frightened cry and dashed into the next room. Pavel Pavlovitch, initially startled, quickly recovered and greeted Velchaninoff with the same overly sweet smile he'd used the night before.

"Alexey Ivanovitch!" he exclaimed in genuine surprise. "Who would have thought it! Come in, come in—sit down! Take the sofa or this chair—sit down, my dear friend! I'll just grab my—" He darted to fetch his coat and threw it on hurriedly, leaving his waistcoat behind.

"No need to stand on ceremony for me," Velchaninoff said, sitting down. "Stay as you are."

"No, no! Excuse me—I must insist on being proper," Pavel Pavlovitch replied, now slightly more presentable. "Well, well! Who would have thought I'd see you here? Not me, that's for sure!"

He perched on the edge of a chair, turning it to face Velchaninoff.

"And why wouldn't you expect me?" Velchaninoff asked. "I told you last night I'd come this morning."

"I thought you wouldn't, sir—truly, I did. After yesterday's visit, I was sure I'd never see you again. I really was."

As they spoke, Velchaninoff glanced around the room. It was a mess. The bed was unmade, clothes were scattered across the floor, and the table held two coffee-stained glasses, a half-empty champagne bottle, and a tumbler beside it. The other room was silent now—the little girl was hiding and as quiet as a mouse.

"You drink champagne at this time of day?" Velchaninoff asked, gesturing toward the bottle.

"It's just leftovers," Pavel Pavlovitch replied, looking a bit embarrassed.

"My goodness! You really have changed."

"Bad habits, sir—picked up all of a sudden. It all started back then. I swear I couldn't stop myself. But I'm fine now—not drunk! I won't babble nonsense like I did last night. Don't worry, sir. It's all under control! I swear, if someone had shown me my current state half a year ago, I wouldn't have believed it. I'd have called them a liar!"

"Hmm. So, you were drunk last night, then?" Velchaninoff asked.

"Yes—I was," admitted Pavel Pavlovitch with a touch of guilt in his voice. "Not exactly drunk, though—just a little past the limit, if you know what I mean! I'm telling you this so you can understand. You see, I'm always worse after drinking. Even if I'm only slightly drunk, the recklessness and lack of reason that come with it linger and make things worse afterward. That's when my grief hits me the hardest. Honestly, I think my grief is what drives me to drink in the first place. When I've had a bit too much, I can be downright foolish and offensive. I'm sure I must have seemed quite strange to you last night."

"Don't you remember what you said and did?" Velchaninoff asked.

"Of course I do—I remember every word and action," Pavel Pavlovitch replied quickly.

"Listen to me, Pavel Pavlovitch," began Velchaninoff, his tone softer now. "I've thought about it, and I've come to much the same conclusion as you seem to have reached. Besides, I think I was a bit too irritable with you last night—too impatient. I admit that freely. The fact is, I'm not always in the best health, and your sudden arrival in the dead of night, well…"

"In the dead of night! You're absolutely right—it was the middle of the night," Pavel Pavlovitch interrupted, nodding his head emphatically. "How on earth I managed to do such a thing, I'll never understand. But let me tell you, I wouldn't have come in if you hadn't opened the door. I would've left just as I came. You know, I actually called on you about a week ago, but you weren't home. After that, I wasn't sure I'd ever try again. You see, Alexey Ivanovitch, I'm a proud man, despite my current state. Every time I saw you in the streets, I thought to myself, 'What if he doesn't recognize me? What if he rejects me after all these years?' Nine years, Alexey Ivanovitch—nine years is no small matter! I didn't dare approach you. I was afraid of being turned away. And yesterday, with that," he gestured toward the champagne bottle, "I lost track of time. It's a good thing you're the kind of man you are, Alexey Ivanovitch, or I'd have no hope of keeping your acquaintance after last night. You remember the old times, don't you?"

Velchaninoff listened carefully. Pavel Pavlovitch's tone seemed earnest, even tinged with a hint of dignity. Yet Velchaninoff couldn't shake the feeling that not a single word from Pavel Pavlovitch's mouth was trustworthy.

"Tell me, Pavel Pavlovitch," Velchaninoff said at last, "I noticed you're not alone here. Whose little girl is that I saw when I came in?"

Pavel Pavlovitch raised his eyebrows in apparent surprise but quickly composed himself. His gaze was open and amiable.

"Whose little girl?" he repeated with a smile. "Why, that's our Liza!"

"Liza?" Velchaninoff asked, his voice faltering slightly. An inexplicable shiver ran through him.

It was a strange, sudden sensation. When he had entered the room and seen the child, he had felt some surprise, but nothing beyond that. Now, however, something deeper was stirring within him—something he couldn't quite name.

"Yes—our Liza, our daughter Liza," Pavel Pavlovitch repeated warmly, his smile widening.

"Your daughter?" Velchaninoff's voice was barely above a whisper. "Do you mean to say that you and Natalia Vasilievna had children?"

"Of course we did! Though, now that I think about it, how could you have known? It happened after you left, Alexey Ivanovitch—our little miracle, sent by Providence!"

Pavel Pavlovitch sprang to his feet, his face lighting up with enthusiasm.

"I never heard a word about it," Velchaninoff murmured, his face growing pale.

"How could you have? How could you?" Pavel Pavlovitch repeated sweetly. "We had lost all hope of children, as you may remember. And then, suddenly, Heaven blessed us with her. Oh, the joy I felt—Heaven alone knows what I felt! It was just a year after you left, I think. No, wait—not quite a year. Let me see... You left us in October or November, didn't you?"

"I left T—— on the twelfth of September," Velchaninoff replied, his voice flat. "I remember the date clearly."

"Ah, September! Dear me, so it was! Well, then—September, October, November, December, January, February, March, April...

May 8th—that's Liza's birthday. Eight months, almost to the day. And if you could've seen her mother—how overjoyed she was—"

"Let me see her. Call her in!" Velchaninoff's words burst out before he could stop them.

"Of course! Right away!" Pavel Pavlovitch exclaimed, hurrying into the adjoining room.

Velchaninoff sat motionless, listening to the hushed but hurried exchange of whispers in the next room. He thought he could hear Liza's small voice, pleading with her father to leave her alone. The sound made his heart ache, though he couldn't explain why.

At last, Pavel Pavlovitch returned, holding Liza by the hand.

"There you go—she's dreadfully shy and proud," he said, beaming. "Just like her mother."

Liza walked into the room quietly, her hand held tightly by her father. Her face was calm, free of tears, but her large blue eyes remained downcast. She was tall for her age, slender, and undeniably pretty. Her delicate features carried an air of seriousness that felt older than her years. For a moment, she hesitated just inside the room, then slowly raised her gaze to glance at Velchaninoff. Her look was fleeting, cautious, almost sullen, and she quickly dropped her eyes again. There was something in her expression that went beyond the usual shyness of a child meeting a stranger. It was as though she harbored an unspoken mistrust or unease that Velchaninoff found deeply unsettling.

Her father led her directly to Velchaninoff. His tone was a mixture of cheerfulness and insistence.

"There now," said Pavel Pavlovitch, guiding her forward. "This gentleman knew your mother very well. He was a good friend of ours. Don't be shy—go on, give him your hand."

Liza gave a small, polite bow and stretched out her hand timidly. There was no warmth in her gesture, only a formality that seemed out of place for a child of her age.

"You see," Pavel Pavlovitch continued with a touch of pride, "Natalia Vasilievna never wanted her to curtsey like most girls. She insisted on teaching her to bow properly, the English way, and to offer her hand as she does now."

As he spoke, Pavel Pavlovitch watched Velchaninoff intently. His gaze was sharp, almost probing, as though he were trying to read Velchaninoff's thoughts. Velchaninoff, however, made no effort to hide his own feelings. He sat frozen, his hand clasping Liza's small one, his eyes fixed on her pale face.

Liza, meanwhile, appeared distracted, her attention fixed solely on her father. She listened carefully to his words, as if trying to gauge his mood or find some hidden meaning in his tone. Her timid demeanor only deepened the strange unease Velchaninoff felt.

Her eyes, large and blue, struck him immediately. They were undeniably familiar, and he recognized them at once. But it wasn't just her eyes that unsettled him. Her pale complexion and the fine texture of her light hair seemed too significant to ignore. These traits, along with the set of her lips, stirred memories of Natalia Vasilievna in a way that made his heart race.

Pavel Pavlovitch, oblivious to Velchaninoff's inner turmoil, launched into a sentimental tale, his voice heavy with emotion. Velchaninoff barely listened, his thoughts consumed by the girl in front of him. Only the concluding words of Pavel Pavlovitch's speech broke through his distracted state.

"... So you can't imagine our joy, Alexey Ivanovitch, when Providence blessed us with this little one. She became everything to me, truly everything. I always felt that if Heaven ever decided to take my other happiness away, I would still have Liza. That's what I clung to, sir, I swear it."

"And Natalia Vasilievna?" Velchaninoff asked abruptly, his voice tinged with a strange intensity.

Pavel Pavlovitch hesitated for a moment, then smiled unevenly, the corner of his mouth twitching upward. "Ah, Natalia Vasilievna," he began, his tone shifting into something lighter but tinged with a hint of bitterness. "You know how she was—she never liked to say much, as you'll remember yourself. Even on her deathbed, she would get cross about the medicines they were giving her. She'd insist it was nothing serious, just a little fever, and that our old doctor Koch could have her fixed up in no time. Why, only five hours before she passed, she was planning a visit to her Aunt—Liza's godmother—at her estate in the country!"

Velchaninoff suddenly stood up, still holding Liza's hand, his expression a mixture of disbelief and something deeper he couldn't quite name. The girl's unwavering gaze on her father seemed to carry a quiet reproach, as though she were silently accusing him of something only she understood.

"Is she unwell?" Velchaninoff asked abruptly, his voice sharp and urgent. The question hung in the air, heavy with unspoken concern, as Pavel Pavlovitch turned to him with a puzzled expression, seemingly caught off guard by the intensity of the inquiry.

"No, I don't think so," said Pavel Pavlovitch, though his tone seemed to carry a hint of uncertainty. "But you can see how we're living here, in this cramped little place. She's a strange child, very sensitive and nervous. Ever since her mother passed away, she hasn't been herself. She was quite ill and hysterical for a whole fortnight after the funeral. Just before you arrived, she was crying her eyes out again, and do you know why? Liza, are you listening to me? You listen! She got herself worked up simply because I was going out and leaving her behind. She insisted that I don't love her as much as I did when her mother was alive. Can you imagine a child like this—at her age—coming up with such ideas? A girl who should still be playing with dolls is sitting here worrying about whether I love her or not! It's absurd! The trouble is, she has no one to play with. There are no other children around."

"Then… are you two completely alone here?" asked Velchaninoff, a frown forming on his face.

"Yes, completely alone," Pavel Pavlovitch admitted, throwing up his hands. "There's a woman who comes in to help once a day, but that's it."

"And when you go out, do you leave her entirely on her own?"

"Of course I do! What else can I do? Yesterday, I locked her in the other room before I left, and that's what all the tears were about this morning. What choice did I have? The day before yesterday, she wandered down to the yard all by herself, and some boy threw a stone at her head. Not only that, but she starts talking to strangers, grabbing at anyone she meets and asking them where I've gone. It's not exactly comforting, you see! But I'll admit, I haven't been very responsible myself. I told her I'd be out for an hour yesterday, and I stayed out until four in the morning. The landlady ended up letting her out by breaking open the door. Imagine how that made me feel! It's all because of this eclipse over my life—this shadow I can't escape!"

"Papa…" Liza's voice was soft and hesitant, filled with a quiet plea.

"Now, don't start that again! What did I tell you yesterday?" Pavel Pavlovitch snapped, his voice sharp.

"I won't! I won't!" Liza cried, clasping her hands together and looking up at him with anxious, pleading eyes.

"This can't continue!" Velchaninoff said, his voice firm and commanding. "Look at you—living in a hole like this when you're a man of means! How can you possibly justify this kind of existence for yourself or her? And the state of this place! It's absolute chaos!"

"This place?" Pavel Pavlovitch echoed, his voice defensive. "We won't be here long. I'm planning to leave within a week—maybe two. And don't think I haven't spent money here already! Yes, I may be 'a man of property,' as you say, but even a man of property has limits!"

"That's enough!" Velchaninoff interrupted, his frustration bubbling over. "I have a proposition for you, and I'm not going to take no for an answer. You just said you'll be here for another week, maybe more. I know a family, the Pogoryeltseffs—Alexander Pavlovitch Pogoryeltseff is a state councillor, a man who could even help you with your business affairs! They're like family to me—I've been close to them for twenty years. Right now, they're at their country villa, which is beautiful. Claudia Petrovna, the lady of the house, is like a sister—or even a mother—to me. They have eight children, Pavel Pavlovitch! Let me take Liza to them. They'll welcome her with open arms. She'll be treated like one of their own daughters. I promise you, they'll adore her!"

Velchaninoff's words came out in a rush, his urgency unmistakable. He was animated, his gestures almost frantic as he tried to convey the sincerity of his offer.

"I'm afraid it's impossible," Pavel Pavlovitch replied, his lips curling into a faint grimace. His eyes met Velchaninoff's, and there was something calculating in his gaze, something that made Velchaninoff's irritation spike.

"Why impossible? What on earth could stop you from letting her go to a place where she'll be safe and cared for?" Velchaninoff demanded.

"Oh, there are many reasons," Pavel Pavlovitch said with a vague shrug. "It's not about you, Alexey Ivanovitch—I trust your intentions completely. But sending her to a strange house, to people of such high standing... I'm not sure they would even want to take her."

"Not want to take her?" Velchaninoff nearly shouted, his voice rising with incredulity. "I told you, I'm like a son to that family! Claudia Petrovna would be overjoyed to have her! She'd treat her as if she were my own child. Stop this nonsense, Pavel Pavlovitch. You're just playing games with me now! What's the point of all this stalling?"

He stamped his foot, his frustration boiling over. The tension in the room was palpable, and Pavel Pavlovitch's evasive demeanor only fueled Velchaninoff's growing impatience.

"No—no, I mean to say—doesn't it seem a bit strange? Shouldn't I call on them a couple of times first? You know, with a house as grand as you say theirs is—don't you think—"

"I'm telling you, it's not grand at all. It's the simplest house in the world," Velchaninoff interrupted, his voice brimming with impatience. "It's not 'smart' in the least. They have a bunch of children running around, and it'll be the best thing for her—it'll turn her into one of them! I'll introduce you myself tomorrow, if that'll make you feel better. Of course, you'll need to thank them and all that once she's there, but you can come along every day with me if you want to check in."

"Oh, but—"

"Stop making excuses! You know it's all nonsense! Now here's the plan: you come to my place tonight—I'll put you up—and we'll head out early tomorrow. By noon, we'll be down there, and it'll all be settled."

"Bless you! You'll really let me stay at your place tonight?" Pavel Pavlovitch exclaimed, his hesitation melting away into unreserved enthusiasm. "You are far too kind! And where is this country house of theirs?"

"It's in the Liesnoy district."

"But, wait—what about her dress? A place like that, you know—a father's heart hesitates—"

"Ridiculous! She's in mourning, isn't she? What else would she wear besides a black dress like this? It's perfect; you couldn't find anything better suited! Maybe just pack her some fresh linen and give her a clean neck-handkerchief."

"Right away, right away. We've just got her linen back from the wash—it won't take a minute to gather it up."

"Great. Now send for a carriage. Can you do that? We need it immediately—no time to waste."

At that moment, an unexpected problem arose: Liza was adamantly opposed to the plan. She had been listening in silence, but her expression revealed mounting terror. Had Velchaninoff glanced at her during his heated conversation with Pavel Pavlovitch, he would have seen the despair etched across her face.

"I won't go," she said quietly but with firm resolve.

"There! Just like her mother!" Pavel Pavlovitch remarked, trying to mask his irritation with a forced laugh.

"I'm not like mamma! I'm not like mamma!" Liza cried, wringing her small hands as tears welled in her eyes. "Oh, papa—papa!" she pleaded, her voice cracking with desperation. Suddenly, she turned and flung herself at Velchaninoff, gripping his arm tightly. "If you take me away—if you leave me—" she began, her voice choked with sobs.

But she didn't get to finish her thought. Pavel Pavlovitch, his patience snapping, grabbed her roughly by the arm and collar. Without a word, he hustled her into the adjoining room, slamming the door shut behind them. Velchaninoff stood frozen, hearing muffled whispers and the subdued sound of Liza crying. He clenched his fists, debating whether to intervene, when the door opened, and Pavel Pavlovitch stepped out.

"She'll come in a moment," he said, forcing a grin that only made his face more unpleasant to look at.

Velchaninoff said nothing. He avoided Pavel Pavlovitch's gaze, fixing his eyes on the far corner of the room instead.

The elderly woman Velchaninoff had encountered earlier on the stairs now appeared, carrying a neatly packed carpetbag with Liza's things. She set it down by the door and turned to Velchaninoff.

"So, you're taking the little lady with you, sir?" she asked, her tone tinged with relief. "If that's the case, you're doing a fine deed. She's a good, quiet child, and you're saving her from—well, from whatever might happen here."

"Oh, come on now, Maria Sisevna—" Pavel Pavlovitch began, his tone defensive.

"Well, what? Tell me I'm wrong! Aren't you ashamed, letting a girl as smart as she is see the kind of things you've got going on here? It's a wonder she hasn't fallen ill from the stress of it all!" The woman's face was flushed with indignation as she gestured sharply toward the chaotic room.

The sound of wheels crunching on the gravel outside interrupted them. "The carriage has arrived for you, sir," the woman said, turning back to Velchaninoff. "It's for Liesnoy, right?"

"Yes, that's right."

"Well then, good luck to you," she added with a small nod, her expression softening just a little as she looked toward the packed bag.

Liza emerged from the room slowly, her small frame tense, her face pale, and her eyes fixed firmly on the floor. She carried her little bag with both hands, clutching it as though it were the only anchor holding her steady. She avoided looking in Velchaninoff's direction entirely, her silence charged with a kind of resistance. There was no outburst this time, no desperate cry, no dramatic clinging to her father. She simply moved with a forced calm, determined not to betray her feelings again.

Pavel Pavlovitch bent down and kissed her lightly on the head, his hand resting awkwardly on her hair for a moment before giving it a perfunctory pat. The gesture was mechanical, devoid of real tenderness, and Liza's reaction was telling. Her lips curled slightly in what could have been either disdain or suppressed pain. Her chin quivered, but she refused to look up at him. She stood stiffly, enduring the moment without a word.

Pavel Pavlovitch's own face had grown pale, and his hands trembled as he reached out to touch her. Velchaninoff could see the man's unease plainly, even though he tried his best not to look at him at all. Velchaninoff's mind was singularly focused—he wanted nothing more than to leave immediately, to put as much distance as possible between himself and this oppressive scene.

When they made their way downstairs, old Maria Sisevna was standing near the entrance, waiting to bid Liza farewell. She embraced the child briefly, murmuring some words of encouragement that neither Velchaninoff nor Pavel Pavlovitch could quite catch. There were more awkward goodbyes and kisses, though none of it seemed to register with Liza, who remained quiet and distant. Her silence had become almost impenetrable.

Liza climbed into the carriage with slow, deliberate movements, as though she were forcing herself to comply. Just as the vehicle was about to pull away, she looked back and caught sight of her father's face. In that instant, her composure cracked. A loud, piercing cry escaped her lips, and she wrung her small hands in desperation. Her body tensed, and for a moment, it seemed as though she might leap out of the carriage altogether.

But before she could act, the carriage lurched forward, its wheels grinding against the stones. The sudden movement threw her back into her seat, and the opportunity to escape was lost. Liza sank into her place, clutching her bag tightly, her face a mask of anguish as she disappeared from view. Pavel Pavlovitch remained standing where he was, pale and trembling, staring after the departing carriage as though he himself had been left behind. Velchaninoff turned away, his only thought to leave this suffocating scene behind as quickly as possible.

Chapter 6

"Are you feeling faint?" Velchaninoff asked hurriedly, his voice shaking with concern. He leaned forward, his eyes scanning Liza's pale face. "Should I tell the driver to stop? We can get you some water."

Liza turned her sharp, accusing eyes on him. There was no trace of the vulnerability he had expected, only anger and mistrust.

"Where are you taking me?" she asked, her voice cold and abrupt, cutting through his attempt at kindness.

"To a very beautiful house, Liza," he replied, trying to sound soothing. "There are so many children there, and they'll all love you. They're the kindest people. Don't be angry with me, Liza. I only want what's best for you."

But his words seemed to fall flat. Liza's expression grew darker, her small hands tightening into fists. Her gaze pierced him with a fiery intensity that made him feel smaller, weaker.

"How—how—how wicked you are!" she burst out, her voice trembling with restrained tears. Her eyes, now flashing with fury, fixed on him accusingly.

"Liza, please listen—" he started, but she cut him off.

"You are bad, bad, and wicked!" she cried, her voice rising. She wrung her hands together as though fighting to keep herself from breaking down entirely.

Velchaninoff felt utterly helpless. "Oh, Liza, Liza," he pleaded, his voice breaking with despair. "If you only knew how much this is hurting me! I'm trying to help you."

Liza's anger didn't waver. She straightened in her seat, her small frame radiating defiance. "Is it true," she asked sharply, "that he is coming tomorrow? Is it true, or are you lying?"

"It's true. I promise you, Liza. I'll bring him down myself. I'll make sure he comes," Velchaninoff answered, desperate to reassure her. His tone was earnest, almost pleading.

"He'll deceive you," she declared, her voice suddenly soft but still bitter. Her eyes dropped to her lap, and her fingers fidgeted nervously with the fabric of her dress. "He always deceives."

Velchaninoff felt a pang of sadness. "Doesn't he love you, Liza?" he asked gently.

"No," came her curt reply, her tone flat and final.

"Has he hurt you, Liza? Has he treated you badly?" he pressed cautiously, his concern mounting.

Liza didn't answer. Her lips tightened, and her eyes avoided his. She turned away and sat quietly, her small frame now drooping with a kind of weary defeat. The silence that hung between them was heavy, oppressive.

Velchaninoff couldn't bear it. He began speaking again, trying to win her over. His words came in a rush—urgent, passionate, even feverish. He told her about the kindness of the family they were going to see, about the joy of being around other children, and about how much he cared for her. He promised her that he would look after her father himself, that he wouldn't let her be hurt again.

At first, Liza's expression didn't change. She listened without trust, her hostility evident in every glance. But she listened. And to Velchaninoff, even that glimmer of attention was a victory. Encouraged, he pressed on, explaining gently but firmly what it meant

61

for a man to drink too much, what it did to a person. He tried to paint a picture of hope, of care, of something better.

When he finally spoke of her mother, something shifted. "I knew your mother well," he said softly. "She was remarkable. She loved you, Liza. She really did."

Liza's eyes, which had remained lowered for so long, suddenly lifted. She looked at him, her gaze fixed and unblinking. Her anger had softened into something else—hesitation, maybe even curiosity.

Velchaninoff continued, speaking carefully now, weaving little stories of her mother, anecdotes of her wit and grace. He described moments that revealed Natalia Vasilievna's strength and love. Little by little, Liza began to respond. At first, her replies were clipped, monosyllabic, her words almost grudging. But gradually, she opened up, though only in fragments.

She admitted, quietly and with obvious reluctance, that she had once loved her father more than her mother. "He used to love me more," she explained, her voice barely audible. "But when Mama died, and I saw her lying there—" Her voice cracked, and she paused, her small hands trembling. "I cried over her. I kissed her face. And since then, I've loved her more than anything. More than everything in the whole world. Every night, I think of her. Every night, I love her."

As she spoke these words, Velchaninoff felt his own heart ache. He held her small hand in his, his grip gentle but firm, and she didn't pull away. The strength of her grief, her love, her little voice trembling with emotion—it all overwhelmed him. In that moment, he resolved that he would do whatever it took to make things better for her, no matter the cost.

Liza, despite her brief openness, soon retreated into her guarded shell. Realizing how much she had revealed, she stopped speaking abruptly. Her silence, coupled with the sharp, distrustful look she gave

Velchaninoff, made it clear that she resented being drawn into sharing her feelings. She gazed at him as though he had tricked her into exposing thoughts she had wanted to keep hidden, and her pride flared up in full force.

By the time their journey was nearing its end, her earlier hysteria had mostly passed, but she remained silent, her mood heavy and sullen. She stared out at her surroundings, her expression closed and brooding, like a small, wary animal in unfamiliar territory. Velchaninoff noticed that her unease wasn't tied to the fact that she was being brought to a strange house. It was something deeper, something that gnawed at her spirit. He sensed that what troubled her most was shame—a deep, bitter shame that her father had given her up so easily. To her, it felt like being discarded, handed over to someone else without a fight.

"She's unwell," Velchaninoff thought with a pang of guilt and anger. "Perhaps seriously so. She's been mistreated and neglected. That drunken, heartless fool!" The thought of Pavel Pavlovitch filled him with fury, and he urged the coachman to hurry. Velchaninoff clung to the hope that the fresh air, the garden, and the company of other children would revive her spirits. He believed with fervor that the new life awaiting her could heal the wounds of the past.

And as for himself, he felt an almost overwhelming sense of purpose swelling within him. It was a feeling so strong, so consuming, that it seemed to breathe new life into his weary soul. "At last, I have something to live for," he thought with sudden clarity. "This is what life is supposed to be—a purpose, a reason to care." He didn't allow himself to get bogged down in details; the larger picture was too beautiful to mar with practicalities. His vision of the future was bright, solid, and untouchable.

The foundation of his plan seemed simple to him. "I'll convince that pitiful drunkard to leave Liza here at the Pogoryeltseffs' house," he thought with determination. "At first, just for a little while, of course. But once she's settled here, she'll stay. She'll belong here. And as for him, he'll be better off alone—he knows it, too. Why else would he treat her like that?" The more he considered it, the more certain he felt that his plan would work.

Finally, the carriage pulled up to the house. It was a charming and welcoming place, surrounded by a garden that seemed alive with color and light. As they came to a stop, a boisterous group of children poured out onto the steps, their cheerful shouts filling the air. Velchaninoff had been a familiar figure in this household for years, and the children greeted him with unrestrained excitement. They adored him, and their enthusiasm was palpable.

"How's the lawsuit going, Uncle Alexey?" the older children teased, their voices carrying mock seriousness. Even the younger ones, too little to understand the joke, joined in, their shrill voices echoing the refrain. It was a running joke in the Pogoryeltseff household to tease Velchaninoff about his ongoing legal troubles, and he couldn't help but smile at their energy.

Liza, however, was less at ease. As she stepped down from the carriage, the children immediately surrounded her, their bright eyes filled with curiosity. They inspected her shyly, their chatter pausing as they took in the unfamiliar newcomer.

Moments later, Claudia Petrovna and her husband emerged to greet them. Claudia, a warm and kind woman in her late thirties, had a radiant smile that made her seem younger than her years. Her husband, Alexander Pavlovitch, though older and more reserved, was the very embodiment of wisdom and kindness. Both greeted Velchaninoff with genuine affection, and, of course, couldn't resist a playful jab about his lawsuit.

This house, this family, had always been more than a refuge to Velchaninoff—it was a true home. Two decades earlier, Claudia Petrovna had almost become his wife. Back then, he had been a young, impulsive university student, swept away by his first experience of love. It had been a fiery and sweet time, though ultimately brief. Claudia had chosen Alexander Pavlovitch, and Velchaninoff had respected her choice. Years later, when their paths crossed again, a deep, enduring friendship had grown between them, free of any lingering bitterness.

In the Pogoryeltseff household, Velchaninoff could be his truest self. Here, he found peace and simplicity, a place where he could laugh, share stories, and even confess his faults without fear of judgment. He had often told Claudia and Alexander that when his years of solitude were behind him, he would settle here for good. And though he had said it lightly, he now realized how much he truly longed for that future.

For now, though, his focus was on Liza. As the children began to draw her out of her shell with their chatter, and Claudia welcomed her with open arms, Velchaninoff felt a cautious hope stir within him. Perhaps, just perhaps, things were beginning to change for the better.

Velchaninoff began by providing the Pogoryeltseffs with the necessary details about Liza, though he chose his words carefully, offering only what he deemed essential. His request to take her in, however, would have been enough without further explanation.

Claudia Petrovna, moved by his account, kissed the little girl gently and reassured Velchaninoff that she would do everything in her power to make Liza feel at home. The children, naturally curious and full of energy, whisked Liza away to play in the garden. Though still visibly hesitant, Liza followed, her small frame disappearing among the boisterous group.

As the minutes passed, Velchaninoff engaged in conversation with Claudia and her husband, but it was clear his mind was elsewhere. His nervous energy did not escape the notice of the Pogoryeltseffs. After a mere half-hour, Velchaninoff rose abruptly, announcing his need to leave. His friends were visibly surprised. They reminded him that he hadn't visited them in weeks, and now, after such a long absence, he was leaving in such haste.

"I'll return tomorrow," Velchaninoff promised with a strained smile, but his urgency was unmistakable.

Claudia Petrovna studied him carefully, sensing there was more on his mind than he was letting on. As if confirming her intuition, Velchaninoff suddenly grasped her hand and, under the guise of needing to share something private about Liza, drew her into another room.

"Do you remember," he began, his voice low and urgent, "what I told you long ago about that year I spent in T——? I shared it only with you, no one else—not even your husband knows the full story."

Claudia nodded, her expression serious. "Yes, of course, I remember. You've mentioned it more than once."

"I didn't just tell you about it," Velchaninoff corrected her, his voice thick with emotion. "I confessed it to you. But I never revealed her name. It was Natalia Vasilievna Trusotsky—this girl's mother. Liza is her child. My child."

Claudia's eyes widened in shock. "Are you absolutely certain of this? Could there be any mistake?" she asked, her tone marked by a mix of disbelief and concern.

"There is no mistake," Velchaninoff insisted, almost breathless. His words tumbled out in a hurried explanation of events, recounting the details with an urgency that left Claudia startled. While she had heard parts of his story before, the revelation of Natalia's identity and Liza's connection to him cast everything in a new light.

For years, Velchaninoff had kept Natalia's name a secret, driven by a deep fear that his friends might one day encounter her and wonder how he could have been so enthralled by such a woman. Even Claudia, his closest confidante, had been kept in the dark—until now.

"And the father—Pavel Pavlovitch—he doesn't know?" Claudia asked, her voice quieter now.

"He knows," Velchaninoff admitted reluctantly. "At least, I think he does. That's the very thing I need to understand. He must know—there's no other explanation. I saw it in his eyes yesterday and again today. But I need to find out how much he knows."

Velchaninoff's pacing quickened as he continued, his emotions spilling over. "He knows all about Bagantoff, but does he know about me? Wives like Natalia—they can deceive their husbands so thoroughly. Even if an angel came down to reveal the truth, the husband would deny it and defend her."

Claudia remained silent, her expression a mixture of compassion and concern.

"I've judged myself for all of this, Claudia. Believe me, I have. But this morning, I was so convinced he knew everything that I let my guard down. I even felt guilty about being rude to him last night. Imagine that! He came to me, not out of friendship, but to flaunt the fact that he knows the truth. And I—fool that I am—I gave him the satisfaction of seeing me flustered."

Velchaninoff's voice grew more intense. "He vents his frustrations on Liza. I can see it. He's hurting her out of spite because she reminds him of everything he's lost. It's infuriating, and it's wrong—but it's human. That's why I need to approach him differently. I need to show him kindness, Claudia. It's the only way. I owe him that much."

Claudia sighed deeply. "Be careful, Alexey Ivanovitch," she said, her tone heavy with worry. "You're so impulsive when you're emotional. I can see how much you care for Liza, and I promise to do my part for her. But tread carefully. There's so much at stake."

When Velchaninoff stepped outside, the Pogoryeltseffs' children had gathered again, laughing and playing. Liza was among them, though she seemed quieter, more subdued. As Velchaninoff kissed her goodbye and promised to return with her father, she remained silent, her gaze avoiding his. But just as he was about to leave, she suddenly grabbed his hand and pulled him aside.

"What is it, Liza?" Velchaninoff asked gently. Her silence stretched on, her wide blue eyes searching his face. The fear and confusion in her expression were unmistakable. She wanted to speak, but the words seemed caught in her throat. Velchaninoff waited, his heart aching at the sight of her struggle.

"He'll hang himself!" she whispered at last, as if speaking in a daze.

"Who will hang himself?" Velchaninoff asked, startled and alarmed.

"He will—him! Last night, he tried to hang himself on a hook," Liza said breathlessly, her words tumbling out in a rush. "I saw it myself! Today, he tried again—he wants to hang himself. He told me so! He said it himself! He's wanted to do it for a long time! I saw it with my own eyes—in the night!"

"That's impossible," Velchaninoff muttered, struggling to believe her words.

Liza suddenly flung herself into his arms, clutching at him desperately. She kissed his hands and burst into tears. Her sobs came in gasps, leaving her unable to catch her breath. She was pleading with him, begging him, but Velchaninoff couldn't make sense of what she was trying to say. Her words were jumbled, her emotions overwhelming.

Velchaninoff would never forget the sight of this distraught child. The image of her tear-streaked face, filled with a desperate and pleading hope, stayed with him always. It haunted his waking moments and invaded his dreams. The way she had clung to him, her last hope in the face of despair, struck him deeply. She had begged him to help her, hysterically praying for his intervention.

"And yet, she cares for him so much!" Velchaninoff thought jealously as his carriage sped back toward town. "She said herself she loved her mother more. Maybe she doesn't love him at all—maybe she even hates him. And what was all that talk about hanging? What did she mean by that? As if he'd actually do it! That idiot wouldn't hang himself! But still, I need to get to the bottom of this. I need to find out everything, settle this whole mess once and for all—and fast!"

Chapter 7

He was desperate to "know everything." Determined not to waste any time, he instructed the coachman to take him straight to Trusotsky's rooms. Yet, midway through the ride, he changed his mind. "Let him come to me instead," he thought. "Meanwhile, I can deal with my cursed law business."

But as the day wore on, he realized he was too distracted to focus on anything. By five o'clock, he decided to head out for dinner. It was then, for the first time, that an amusing thought struck him. What if, by constantly meddling and chasing after his lawyer, he was only making things worse for his case? What if his lawyer avoided him on purpose? Velchaninoff laughed heartily at the idea. "If I'd thought of this in the evening, instead of now, I'd be fuming with rage!" he mused, laughing even more.

Despite his moment of humor, his thoughts grew heavier, his impatience deeper. He couldn't settle on any task, nor could he figure out what troubled him most. "I need that man here!" he finally concluded. "I have to unravel his mystery first. Then I'll know what to do. There's a duel brewing here!"

When he returned home around seven, Pavel Pavlovitch was nowhere to be seen. First, Velchaninoff was surprised. Then irritation set in, followed by disappointment, and finally, an unsettling fear. "God knows how this will end!" he muttered, alternating between flinging himself onto the sofa and pacing restlessly around the room. Every few minutes, his eyes darted to the clock, the seconds crawling by.

At last, around nine o'clock, Pavel Pavlovitch arrived.

"If he meant to unsettle me, he couldn't have done it better!" thought Velchaninoff, though he felt an undeniable wave of relief wash over him at the sight of his guest.

Velchaninoff greeted him warmly, asking why he was so late. Pavel Pavlovitch responded with a disagreeable smile. He sauntered into the room with an air of casual indifference, tossed his crape-adorned hat onto a chair, and made himself comfortable. Velchaninoff noticed this careless attitude—it was nothing like the Pavel Pavlovitch of the previous evening.

Keeping his tone calm, Velchaninoff began to recount what he had done with Liza. He explained how warmly she had been welcomed, how good the change would be for her, and then subtly shifted the topic to the Pogoryeltseffs. He avoided mentioning Liza directly again, instead talking about the family's kindness and his long-standing relationship with them.

Pavel Pavlovitch listened with a detached air, occasionally glancing at Velchaninoff with a faintly mocking expression from beneath his lashes.

"You're such an enthusiast," he muttered finally, his tone dripping with sarcasm and his smile distinctly unpleasant.

"You seem to be in a foul mood today," Velchaninoff remarked irritably.

"And why shouldn't I be as nasty as everyone else?" Pavel Pavlovitch suddenly exclaimed. He spoke so abruptly and with such intensity that it seemed as though he had been lying in wait, ready to pounce on the first opportunity to lash out.

"Go ahead, do as you like," Velchaninoff laughed. "I only thought something might have upset you!"

"Well, it has!" Pavel Pavlovitch exclaimed, as if proud of the fact.

71

"What is it, then?" Velchaninoff asked.

Pavel Pavlovitch paused for a moment before answering.

"It's that Stepan Michailovitch Bagantoff—our dear friend!—up to his usual tricks. He's a real star in the high circles of society, isn't he?" he said, his voice dripping with sarcasm.

"Did he refuse to see you again? Or what happened this time?"

"No, not quite," Pavel Pavlovitch replied, dragging out his words. "This time, they actually let me in. I had the honor of seeing him up close, too—only he happened to be a corpse, that's all."

"What? Bagantoff is dead?" Velchaninoff asked, startled. Though, on second thought, there wasn't much reason for him to feel so surprised.

"Yes, my 'faithful friend' of six years is dead!" Pavel Pavlovitch sneered. "Died yesterday, sometime around midday. I didn't even know about it! Maybe he died right as I was visiting—who knows? The funeral is tomorrow. He's lying in his coffin as we speak. They said it was nervous fever. And they let me in, they really did! I told them I was an old friend, so they allowed me to go and admire his features. Such a delightful trick for a dear friend to play on me! Imagine—I might've come to St. Petersburg just for him!"

"Well, there's no point in being angry at him for it, is there? It's not like he died on purpose," Velchaninoff replied with a chuckle.

"Oh, but I speak out of pure sympathy. He was such a dear friend! Oh, such a very dear friend!" Pavel Pavlovitch said, his smile filled with a sly and detestable irony.

"You know, Alexey Ivanovitch," he continued, his tone suddenly changing, "I think you ought to treat me to something. I treated you often enough, didn't I? Back in T——, I was your host every single day for a whole year. Come on, send for a bottle of wine—my throat is terribly dry."

"With pleasure! Why didn't you say so earlier? What would you like?" Velchaninoff asked.

"Not 'you,'" Pavel Pavlovitch corrected him, his tone defiant but his eyes showing a hint of caution as they met Velchaninoff's. "Say 'we.' Of course, we'll drink together!"

"Shall we get champagne?"

"Of course! It's not time for vodka yet!" Pavel Pavlovitch replied with a smirk.

Velchaninoff stood up slowly, rang the bell, and gave Mavra the necessary orders.

"We'll drink to this happy reunion after nine long years apart!" Pavel Pavlovitch declared with an inappropriate giggle. "Why, you're the only true friend I have left now! Bagantoff is gone. It's just like the poet said:

'Great Patroclus is no more,

Mean Thersites liveth yet.'

—and so on, don't you know?"

As he said the name "Thersites," Pavel Pavlovitch touched his own chest in a theatrical gesture.

"I wish you'd just speak plainly, you miserable fellow," Velchaninoff thought to himself. "I can't stand these hints!" His temper, which he had been struggling to control for a while now, was starting to flare.

"Tell me something," Velchaninoff said at last. "If you think Bagantoff wronged you—and clearly you do—shouldn't you be glad he's dead? What's making you so angry?"

"Glad? Why should I be glad?" Pavel Pavlovitch asked.

"I'm judging based on what I imagine your feelings might be."

"Well, you're wrong this time," Pavel Pavlovitch replied with a bitter laugh. "As a certain sage once said, 'My good enemy is dead, but I have an even better one still alive.' Ha-ha!"

"Well, you spent five years looking at him while he was alive—surely that was enough time to study his face!" Velchaninoff said sharply, his voice full of irritation and disdain.

"Yes, but how was I supposed to know then, sir?" Pavel Pavlovitch snapped back, as if leaping out from a hiding place he had been waiting in. He seemed thrilled to be asked a question he had clearly anticipated for some time. "What do you take me for, Alexey Ivanovitch?" At that moment, a new expression crossed his face, one that completely altered the previous malicious and unpleasant look.

"Do you mean to tell me you knew nothing about it?" Velchaninoff asked in surprise.

"Knew nothing? As if I could have known and—oh, you proud lot! You think of people as if they're no better than dogs, and you measure everyone by your own standards." Pavel Pavlovitch slammed his fist down on the table with a loud thud, only to look startled at his own outburst.

Velchaninoff's face brightened suddenly.

"Listen, Pavel Pavlovitch," he said, his tone calm but pointed. "It doesn't make the slightest difference to me whether you knew or didn't know about it. If you didn't, that's even more to your credit. But—I don't see why you've chosen me to share all this with."

"I wasn't talking about you," Pavel Pavlovitch muttered, staring at the floor. "Don't get upset—it wasn't about you."

Just then, Mavra entered the room with the champagne.

"Here it is!" Pavel Pavlovitch exclaimed, lighting up with delight at the sight of the bottle. "Now then, tumblers, my good girl—fetch us some tumblers, quickly! Excellent! Thank you, we won't need you anymore, dear Mavra. Oh, you've already drawn the cork? Marvelous! Well, off you go now—ta-ta!"

The arrival of the champagne seemed to bolster Pavel Pavlovitch's confidence. He turned to Velchaninoff with a faintly defiant expression.

"Admit it," he said with a sudden giggle, "you're dying to hear all about this, and it's definitely not 'the same to you,' as you claim! Be honest—you'd be miserable if I got up and left right now without telling you anything more."

"Not in the slightest," Velchaninoff replied coolly. "I assure you."

Pavel Pavlovitch smiled knowingly, a look that seemed to say, "You're lying."

"Well, let's get down to it," Pavel Pavlovitch said, pouring champagne into two glasses.

"Here's a toast," he went on, raising his glass. "To the health and peace in Paradise of our dearly departed friend Bagantoff."

He raised his glass and drank.

"I'm not drinking to that," Velchaninoff said firmly, placing his glass back on the table.

"Why not? It's a perfectly fine toast."

"Tell me, were you drunk when you came here?" Velchaninoff asked, leaning forward slightly.

"Maybe just a little. Why?" Pavel Pavlovitch replied, his tone casual but with a flicker of amusement in his eyes.

"Oh—nothing specific. It's just that it seemed like yesterday, and especially this morning, you were genuinely upset about the loss of Natalia Vasilievna."

"And who says I'm not upset now?" snapped Pavel Pavlovitch suddenly, as though someone had pressed a button to make him spit out the words like a mechanical toy.

"No, no, I'm not saying that," replied Velchaninoff. "But surely you must admit, you might be mistaken about Bagantoff. That's no small matter."

Pavel Pavlovitch smirked and gave a sly wink.

"Ah, wouldn't you just love to know how I figured out everything about Bagantoff, huh?"

Velchaninoff flushed.

"I've told you already, it doesn't matter to me," he replied curtly, though his reddening face betrayed otherwise. To himself, he added, "Maybe I should just toss him and the bottle out of the window." His face grew hotter with every word.

Pavel Pavlovitch poured himself another glass, his smirk widening.

"I'll tell you right away how I uncovered all there was to know about Mr. Bagantoff. I can see you're dying to hear it—your curiosity is practically burning you up, Alexey Ivanovitch. You're such a fiery man—oh, dreadfully fiery! Ha-ha-ha. But first, hand me a cigarette, would you? Ever since March, you know—"

"Here's a cigarette," interrupted Velchaninoff, handing him one impatiently.

"Ever since March, I've been a ruined man," Pavel Pavlovitch continued, becoming increasingly familiar in his tone. "And here's how it all started. You know, consumption is a fascinating illness," he began with a strange, almost casual air. "You watch someone dying of it, and you'd never guess that tomorrow will be their last day. I told you before how Natalia Vasilievna, right up until five hours before she passed, was still talking about visiting her aunt in two weeks. Well, some people—you know this, I'm sure—have the awful habit of hoarding old junk, like love letters and whatnot. Instead of burning those scraps of paper, they save every last one, sorting and tying them into neat little bundles. Why? Maybe they think it'll bring them comfort later on, I don't know."

He leaned back dramatically and continued. "Since she was so certain old Doctor Koch would cure her, Natalia Vasilievna didn't expect to die. So, when she passed, she left behind a beautiful little black desk in her bureau—oh, it was a stunning piece! Inlaid with mother-of-pearl and bound in silver, complete with a lock and key. It had belonged to her grandmother."

Pavel Pavlovitch paused for effect before going on. "And in this box, my dear sir, was everything—everything from the past twenty years, down to the day and hour. And since Mr. Bagantoff fancied himself a writer—why, the man had even published a melodramatic novel in some newspaper once—it was no surprise to find a hundred or so of his 'literary masterpieces' tucked away in that box. These little gems spanned five whole years."

He chuckled maliciously and added, "What's more, some of those brilliant works were marked with Natalia Vasilievna's own notes—written in pencil, no less! A real treasure for a loving husband's heart, don't you think?"

77

Velchaninoff quickly thought back to the past and recalled that he had never written a single letter or note directly to Natalia Vasilievna. The only letters he had written from St. Petersburg were addressed jointly to both Mr. and Mrs. Trusotsky, as they had agreed beforehand. He had never even replied to Natalia Vasilievna's final letter, the one in which she dismissed him completely.

After finishing his speech, Pavel Pavlovitch fell silent. He sat there for a full minute, grinning in a way that made Velchaninoff feel sick.

"Why don't you answer my question, my friend?" Pavel Pavlovitch asked at last, breaking the silence. His tone hinted at frustration with Velchaninoff's lack of response.

"What question?" Velchaninoff replied sharply.

"Why, the question about how delightful it must have been for me, as a devoted husband, to open that desk and see all that evidence."

"Your feelings are none of my business," Velchaninoff snapped bitterly, standing up and beginning to pace the room.

"I bet you're thinking right now, 'What kind of disgusting man parades his humiliation like this?' Ha-ha! My, how sensitive and high-minded you are, Alexey Ivanovitch!"

"Not at all," Velchaninoff replied coldly. "I wasn't thinking that. On the contrary, I think you're—well, aside from being drunk—a man so shaken by the death of someone who wronged you that you're not yourself. I completely understand your frustration, and I even sympathize with your wish that Bagantoff were still alive. I respect that. But—"

"And why do you assume I want Bagantoff to still be alive?" Pavel Pavlovitch interrupted, narrowing his eyes.

"Oh, that's your business," Velchaninoff replied, shrugging.

"I'll bet anything you're thinking about a duel!" Pavel Pavlovitch exclaimed with a sly grin.

"Damn it, sir!" Velchaninoff burst out, barely holding back his temper. "I was thinking that, like any respectable person in your situation, you would handle this directly and with dignity, instead of degrading yourself with these ridiculous jokes, sneers, and complaints. They only make things worse for you. I thought you'd act like a man with some self-respect."

"Ha-ha-ha! But what if I'm not a respectable person?" Pavel Pavlovitch retorted, his grin widening.

"Well, if that's the case, then why the hell would you even care about Bagantoff being alive?" Velchaninoff shot back.

"Oh, my dear sir," Pavel Pavlovitch said, his grin turning sly. "I would've liked to sit down with him, have a nice chat, and share a bottle of wine—just like old friends."

"He wouldn't have drunk with you," Velchaninoff said flatly.

"And why not? Noblesse oblige? You're drinking with me, aren't you? What makes him better than you?"

"I'm not drinking with you," Velchaninoff replied, his voice cold.

"What's with the sudden pride?" Pavel Pavlovitch sneered.

Velchaninoff suddenly laughed—a sharp, nervous laugh that echoed through the room.

"Good grief!" he exclaimed. "You're nothing like what I thought you were. I always imagined you as just a 'permanent husband,' but now I see you're more like a bird of prey."

"What's that supposed to mean? 'Permanent husband?' What's a 'permanent husband?'" Pavel Pavlovitch asked, his interest piqued.

"Oh, it's just a type of husband, that's all," Velchaninoff replied dismissively. "It would take too long to explain. Anyway, it's time for you to leave. I'm sick of you."

"And the 'bird of prey' part—what did you mean by that?" Pavel Pavlovitch pressed, leaning forward eagerly.

"I said it as a joke," Velchaninoff replied with a wave of his hand.

"Still, tell me—what exactly did you mean by 'bird of prey,' Alexey Ivanovitch? Please, I want to understand," Pavel Pavlovitch persisted, his tone now almost pleading.

Velchaninoff suddenly shouted, his voice rising sharply, "That's enough of this! It's time for you to leave. Get out of here, will you?"

"No, sir, it's not enough!" Pavel Pavlovitch shouted back, standing up with a sudden burst of energy. "Even if you're tired of me, it's still not enough. You have to drink with me first and clink glasses. I'm not leaving until you do! No, no! Not until we drink together."

"Pavel Pavlovitch, will you leave or not? Go to the devil!" Velchaninoff retorted angrily.

"With pleasure, Alexey Ivanovitch. I'll go straight to the devil if you want—but not before we drink! You might not want to drink with me, but I want to drink with you. And not just drink—I want to drink with you properly."

Pavel Pavlovitch was no longer laughing or grinning. His face changed completely, as did the tone of his voice. It was as though he had become a different person, and Velchaninoff found himself stunned by the sudden transformation.

"Come on, Alexey Ivanovitch. Let's drink—don't refuse me!" Pavel Pavlovitch said, gripping Velchaninoff's hand tightly and looking into his eyes with an intense expression. It was clear there was more to this request than simply sharing a drink.

Velchaninoff hesitated, muttering, "But there's only dregs left."

"There's still enough for a couple of glasses—it's clear enough. Now, take your glass, and I'll take mine. Let's clink glasses and drink together." Pavel Pavlovitch handed Velchaninoff a glass, and they touched them together before drinking.

"Oh, Alexey Ivanovitch! Now that we've drunk together—" Pavel Pavlovitch suddenly raised a hand to his forehead and sat silently for a moment, as though something profound had overcome him.

Velchaninoff felt a shiver of anticipation. He thought Pavel Pavlovitch was finally going to reveal everything. But instead, Pavel Pavlovitch just sat there, smiling at him with that familiar, irritatingly sly grin.

"What do you want from me, you drunken fool?" Velchaninoff shouted, furious. He stamped his foot hard on the floor. "You're just toying with me!"

"Calm down—why are you yelling?" Pavel Pavlovitch replied, raising his voice slightly but keeping his tone steady. "I'm not playing games with you. Do you know what you mean to me now?" Suddenly, he grabbed Velchaninoff's hand and kissed it before Velchaninoff could react.

"There. That's what you mean to me. And now, I'll leave for the devil."

"Wait! Hold on!" Velchaninoff called out, snapping out of his stunned state. "There's something I need to say to you."

Pavel Pavlovitch paused at the door and turned back.

"You need to come with me tomorrow to the Pogoryeltseffs," Velchaninoff said, looking away awkwardly. "You should thank them and get to know them."

"Of course, of course," Pavel Pavlovitch replied immediately, waving his hand in agreement as if this were obvious and didn't need saying.

"And Liza's expecting you. I promised her," Velchaninoff added.

"Liza?" Pavel Pavlovitch turned sharply, his tone rising with emotion. "Liza? Do you know what this girl means to me—what she has meant and still means?" His voice grew louder and more impassioned. "But no, not now! We'll discuss that later. For now, Alexey Ivanovitch, it's not enough that we've drunk together. There's something more I need—something else I must have!"

With that, he placed his hat on a nearby chair and stood still, breathing heavily. His eyes bore into Velchaninoff with the same fiery intensity as before.

Alexey Ivanovitch was taken aback. Pavel Pavlovitch leaned closer, his breath heavy with the sharp, unpleasant smell of wine.

"Now, now!" Pavel Pavlovitch exclaimed with drunken excitement, his eyes wild. "Let me tell you something! I thought back then, 'Surely not him too! If this man—if even this man is guilty—then who can I ever trust again?'"

With that, Pavel Pavlovitch suddenly broke into tears.

"Do you see now? Do you understand? This is how much you mean to me as a friend," he said, his voice trembling. Without another word, he grabbed his hat and dashed out of the room.

For several minutes, Velchaninoff stood frozen, just as he had after Pavel Pavlovitch's first visit.

"It's just drunken nonsense," he muttered to himself at last. "That's all it is—nothing more!" he repeated as he undressed and lay down in his bed.

Chapter 8

The next morning, Velchaninoff paced back and forth in his room, sipping his coffee as he waited for Pavel Pavlovitch. They had arranged to leave early to visit the Pogoryeltseffs together. However, Velchaninoff couldn't shake the feeling that he'd woken up with the memory of being slapped the night before.

"He knows everything far too well," he thought anxiously. "He's going to take it out on me through Liza!" The image of the little girl flashed vividly in his mind, making his heart race with anticipation. He told himself that in just a couple of hours, he would see his precious Liza again. "Yes, no doubt about it," he thought. "She's my whole life now! What does anything else matter—those 'memories,' that slap, any of it? My whole past has been nothing but pain and struggle. But now—now everything is different!"

Despite his excitement, darker thoughts crept in.

"He's tormenting me through Liza, that's obvious. He mistreats her to get back at me—for everything!" Velchaninoff blushed deeply as he remembered Pavel Pavlovitch's behavior the night before. "I can't allow him to behave like that again. It's nearly half-past eleven, and still no sign of him."

By the time the clock struck twelve-thirty, Velchaninoff's impatience had turned into outright distress. Pavel Pavlovitch still hadn't shown up. Slowly, he began to suspect that Pavel Pavlovitch had no intention of coming back. The realization left him in despair. "That wretch knows I'm counting on him! What am I supposed to do about Liza now? How can I show up without him?"

Unable to wait any longer, Velchaninoff decided to go to the Pokrofsky Hotel at one o'clock to find Pavel Pavlovitch himself.

When he arrived, he was told that Pavel Pavlovitch hadn't been home all night. He had stopped by briefly at nine in the morning but had left again after only fifteen minutes.

Standing in the doorway, Velchaninoff listened to the servants' account. Mechanically, he reached for the door handle, then stopped himself and asked for Maria Sisevna.

She came promptly. Maria was an older woman, kind-hearted and warm, as Velchaninoff would later describe her to Claudia Petrovna. After answering his questions about yesterday's journey with Liza, she began sharing her own stories about Pavel Pavlovitch.

She told Velchaninoff that she would have thrown him out long ago if it weren't for the child. Pavel Pavlovitch had already been kicked out of the hotel for his bad behavior. "Oh, he does awful things!" Maria said. "Imagine him telling the poor child, in a fit of anger, that she wasn't his daughter, but—"

"No, no! That's impossible!" Velchaninoff interrupted, horrified.

Maria Sisevna's voice was trembling as she recounted her story. "I heard it myself! Of course, she's just a child, but you can't say things like that around a clever little girl like her! She was so upset—cried her heart out. Not long ago, we had a terrible incident here. Some delivery man or someone like that rented a room in the evening, and by morning, he'd hanged himself. They said he'd run off with stolen money. The house was packed with people coming to gawk at him. Pavel Pavlovitch wasn't home at the time, but the child got out and wandered around. She ended up going with the crowd to see the body. I saw her staring at the poor man with the strangest expression and dragged her away immediately, of course. But she was trembling so badly, I could barely get her back to the apartment. As soon as we were home, she fainted dead away, and it was all I could do to bring her around. I don't know if she's got some kind of epilepsy or what—but she's been unwell ever since.

"When her father found out, he pinched her all over. He doesn't hit her—he just pinches her like that. Then he went off, got drunk, and came back to scare her. He told her, 'I'm going to hang myself too, all because of you. I'll hang myself right there on that curtain cord.' He even made a loop in the string while she watched. The poor little thing was beside herself, clinging to him and crying, 'I'll be good! I'll be good!' It was heartbreaking, truly it was!"

Velchaninoff, though braced for shocking tales about Pavel Pavlovitch, was utterly stunned by these revelations. He could hardly believe his ears.

Maria Sisevna went on with more horrifying anecdotes. Once, she said, if she hadn't been nearby, Liza would have thrown herself out of the window. On another occasion, Pavel Pavlovitch had stormed out of the room, slurring to himself, "I'll smash her head in with a stick! I'll kill her like a dog!" He had walked off, muttering the same dreadful threats over and over.

Overwhelmed, Velchaninoff called for a carriage and set off toward the Pogoryeltseffs' estate. But before he left the city, his carriage came to a halt at a busy crossroads near a small bridge. A long funeral procession was passing, causing a traffic jam. Both sides of the bridge were crowded with waiting carriages and pedestrians.

It was clear the funeral was for someone of significance; the procession stretched on with a mix of private carriages and hired ones. Suddenly, Velchaninoff caught sight of a familiar face in the window of one of the carriages. It was Pavel Pavlovitch.

At first, Velchaninoff thought he must be mistaken, but then Pavel Pavlovitch nodded at him and smiled, even going so far as to kiss his hand theatrically from the window.

Velchaninoff leaped out of his carriage. Ignoring the press of people and the shouts of policemen, he forced his way through the crowd to Pavel Pavlovitch's carriage. He found him sitting inside, entirely alone.

"What are you doing here?" Velchaninoff demanded. "Why didn't you come to my house? What's going on?"

Pavel Pavlovitch grinned and replied with a giggle, "I'm settling a debt. Don't shout! I'm here to pay my respects."

"Paying respects? What nonsense is this?" Velchaninoff exclaimed, growing more furious. "Get out of there and come with me! Now!"

"I can't leave—it's a debt I must repay."

"Then I'll drag you out myself!" Velchaninoff shouted.

Pavel Pavlovitch giggled again, still in good spirits. "Then I'll scream, sir! I'll scream!" His tone was mocking, as if it were all a joke, but he still slid further into the corner of the carriage.

"Step back, sir, you're going to get run over!" a policeman warned.

A carriage attempting to merge into the funeral procession caused a brief commotion, forcing Velchaninoff to step aside. The press of the crowd and carriages soon separated him from Pavel Pavlovitch altogether. Frustrated, Velchaninoff shrugged, turned back, and climbed into his own vehicle.

Velchaninoff couldn't shake his anger and disgust as he reflected on the situation. "It doesn't matter. I couldn't take someone like him with me, no matter what," he muttered, still trembling from the frustration and revulsion he felt. Later, when he shared Maria Sisevna's story and the encounter at the funeral with Claudia Petrovna, she listened intently, her expression growing serious.

"I'm worried about you," she finally said. "You need to cut ties with that man—and the sooner, the better."

"He's just a drunk fool!" Velchaninoff exclaimed, his voice heated. "Why should I be afraid of him? Besides, how can I break things off with him? What about Liza?"

Meanwhile, Liza was unwell. A fever had taken hold of her the night before, and an esteemed doctor had been summoned from town earlier that morning. The news left Velchaninoff deeply unsettled. Claudia Petrovna led him to see the sick girl.

"I watched her closely yesterday," Claudia said, pausing outside Liza's door. "She's a proud, troubled child. She's ashamed—ashamed to be here, ashamed because her father has abandoned her. I believe that's the root of her illness."

"Abandoned her? Why do you think he's abandoned her?" Velchaninoff asked, startled.

"Think about it," she replied. "He let her come here—to a strange house—with a man who, if not a complete stranger, is hardly someone he has a solid relationship with."

"But I brought her here myself—almost against his will," Velchaninoff protested.

Inside the room, Liza didn't seem surprised to see Velchaninoff alone. She gave him a faint, bitter smile and turned her flushed face toward the wall. She said nothing in response to his heartfelt promises to bring her father the next day or his awkward attempts to comfort her.

When Velchaninoff left the room, he broke down and wept.

The doctor finally arrived in the evening. His first words struck fear into everyone: he regretted not being called sooner. When told that the child had only fallen ill the previous night, he expressed disbelief.

"It all depends on how she gets through tonight," he said gravely after examining her. He made the necessary arrangements before departing, promising to return early the next morning.

Velchaninoff wanted to stay the night, but Claudia Petrovna insisted he make another attempt to fetch Pavel Pavlovitch.

"Try again!" she urged.

"Try again?" Velchaninoff exclaimed, his voice filled with passion. "I'll tie him up if I have to and drag him here myself!"

The thought of physically hauling Pavel Pavlovitch back filled him with impatient energy.

"I don't feel the least bit guilty toward him anymore," he declared to Claudia as he prepared to leave. "I take back every apologetic word I said yesterday—all of it!"

In Liza's room, she lay with her eyes closed as if sleeping. She seemed calmer. Velchaninoff leaned over her gently, intending to kiss even just the edge of her bedding, when she suddenly opened her eyes, as though waiting for him.

"Take me away," she whispered softly.

Her words carried no anger, only quiet sadness, and an understanding that her request couldn't be granted. Velchaninoff, heartbroken, tried to explain gently why it wasn't possible. Without replying, she closed her eyes again, shutting herself off from him as though he weren't there.

Once back in town, Velchaninoff directed his coachman to take him to the Pokrofsky. It was already ten o'clock at night. Pavel

Pavlovitch wasn't at his lodgings. Velchaninoff paced the hallway for half an hour, consumed by restless frustration. Maria Sisevna eventually informed him that Pavel Pavlovitch wasn't expected back until the early hours of the morning.

"Fine! Then I'll come back before dawn!" Velchaninoff declared, practically beside himself, before heading back to his own home.

When he reached his building, Mavra met him at the gate with surprising news. "That visitor from yesterday has been waiting for you since just before ten," she said.

"What?" Velchaninoff exclaimed in disbelief.

"He even had some tea," she added, "and he sent me out to buy more wine—the same kind as yesterday. He gave me the money himself."

Chapter 9

Pavel Pavlovitch had made himself quite comfortable. He was sitting in the same chair he had used the day before, smoking a cigar, and pouring the last tumbler of champagne from the bottle. A teapot and a half-empty glass of tea sat on the table next to him. His flushed face radiated a cheerful, almost exaggerated friendliness. He had taken off his coat and was lounging in his shirt sleeves.

"Forgive me, my dearest friend," he exclaimed when he saw Velchaninoff enter, quickly grabbing his coat to put it back on. "I took it off to really relax."

Velchaninoff approached him with a threatening look.

"You're not completely drunk yet, are you? Can you understand what I'm saying?"

Pavel Pavlovitch seemed momentarily flustered.

"No, not completely drunk. I was just thinking about the dear departed, but no, not quite drunk yet."

"Can you understand what I'm telling you?"

"My dear sir, I came here specifically to listen to you."

"Fine," Velchaninoff shouted, raising his voice. "Then I'll start by saying you're an idiot, sir!"

"If you're starting like this, I can only imagine how you'll finish!" Pavel Pavlovitch replied, clearly uneasy.

Velchaninoff ignored him and roared again, "Your daughter is very sick—she's in danger! Have you abandoned her entirely, or not?"

"Oh, surely she's not dying yet?"

"I'm telling you she's very sick. Dangerously sick."

"What is it, fits? Or—"

"Don't spout nonsense. She's gravely ill. You need to go see her, if for no other reason than that."

"To thank your friends, you mean? To show my gratitude for their hospitality? Of course, I understand, Alexey Ivanovitch—my dearest friend!" Pavel Pavlovitch suddenly grabbed Velchaninoff's hands, his voice thick with drunken sentiment. His eyes filled with tears as he added, "Alexey Ivanovitch, don't yell at me—please don't shout! If you do, I might throw myself into the Neva. Who knows? We have so many important things to discuss. There's plenty of time to visit the Pogoryeltseffs another day."

Velchaninoff struggled to keep his temper in check. "You're drunk, and because of that, I can't even make sense of what you're trying to say," he replied coldly. "But let me make this clear: I'm prepared to have a real conversation with you anytime, the sooner the better. However, first, let me tell you what's going to happen. I'm going to make sure you stay put. You'll sleep here tonight, and tomorrow I'm taking you to see Liza. I won't let you get away again. If necessary, I'll tie you up and carry you there myself. Do you understand? Now, how do you like this sofa for sleeping on?" Velchaninoff pointed to a wide, soft divan across from his own.

"Oh, anything will do for me!" Pavel Pavlovitch replied.

"Good. Then this will be your bed," Velchaninoff said, pulling sheets, blankets, and a pillow from a cupboard and tossing them to his guest. "Here you go—now make your bed. Get to it!"

Pavel Pavlovitch stood in the middle of the room, his arms full of bedding, a silly, drunken grin on his face. He seemed unsure of what to do until Velchaninoff barked at him again to hurry up. At that, he began awkwardly preparing the divan, pushing the table out of the way and smoothing the sheet over the cushions. Velchaninoff stepped in to assist, feeling a grim satisfaction in seeing his guest's nervous compliance.

"Now, drink that wine and lie down!" Velchaninoff commanded. He felt an irresistible urge to order this man around. "I suppose you decided to order this wine on your own, didn't you?"

"Yes, I did, Alexey Ivanovitch! I sent for the wine because I knew you wouldn't bother to send for any more yourself," replied Pavel Pavlovitch.

"Well, it's good that you knew that. But I want you to understand something else. I've made up my mind—I'm not going to tolerate any more of your ridiculous behavior."

"Oh, I fully understand, Alexey Ivanovitch. That sort of thing could only happen once," Pavel Pavlovitch said with a weak giggle.

Velchaninoff, who had been pacing back and forth across the room, stopped abruptly in front of him.

"Pavel Pavlovitch," he said seriously, "speak honestly. You're a smart man—I admit that—but you're on the wrong track here. Speak openly, like an honest person, and I promise, on my word of honor, that I'll answer all your questions."

Pavel Pavlovitch gave his usual unpleasant grin, the one that always infuriated Velchaninoff.

"Wait!" Velchaninoff shouted. "No games this time—I see right through you. I'm telling you again, I swear on my honor to answer anything you want to ask and to give you whatever kind of explanation you need, reasonable or not. I wish you could understand me!"

"Well, since you're being so kind," Pavel Pavlovitch began cautiously, leaning slightly toward him, "I'd like to know more about what you said yesterday about 'bird of prey.'"

Velchaninoff spat on the ground in sheer frustration and resumed pacing the room even faster than before.

"No, no, Alexey Ivanovitch! Don't dismiss my question. You don't understand how curious I am about it. I swear, I came here just to ask you this. I know I'm not speaking clearly, but bear with me. I've seen the phrase before. Tell me, was Bagantoff a 'bird of prey,' or not? How can you tell the difference?"

Velchaninoff continued walking back and forth, refusing to respond for several moments.

"A bird of prey," he finally said, stopping in front of Pavel Pavlovitch and speaking with intensity, "is someone who would poison Bagantoff while pretending to drink champagne with him as a friend, just like you did with me yesterday. Instead of escorting his miserable body to the cemetery—as you did, for some twisted, petty reason— you'd be revealing your true nature, which is even lower and more despicable than it already is. Yes, your actions turn back on you and make you even viler."

"You're right, I shouldn't have gone," Pavel Pavlovitch agreed meekly. "But don't you think you're being a bit—"

"A bird of prey," Velchaninoff interrupted, "is not someone who rehearses their grievances like a school lesson, whining and posing, burdening others with their self-pity. That's just pathetic. By the way, is it true you wanted to hang yourself? Answer me—is it true or not?"

"I—I don't know. Maybe I thought about it when I was drunk—I don't remember," Pavel Pavlovitch stammered. "You see, Alexey Ivanovitch, poisoning someone wouldn't be suitable for me. I hold a high position, I have money, and I might want to remarry someday—who knows?"

"Yes, and getting sent to Siberia would complicate things for you, wouldn't it?" Velchaninoff said sharply.

"Of course, though they say hard labor isn't as bad as it used to be. But you've reminded me of a story, Alexey Ivanovitch," said Pavel Pavlovitch, leaning forward with a drunken grin. "I thought of it while riding here and meant to share it with you later. Do you remember Liftsoff from T——? He came around while you were there. His younger brother, quite an important fellow, was serving under the governor at L——. One day, this brother quarreled with Colonel Golubenko in front of some ladies—especially one lady in particular. Liftsoff felt deeply insulted but kept it to himself. Meanwhile, Golubenko proposed to that same lady, and she accepted him.

"Now imagine this: Liftsoff became great friends with Golubenko after that, even offering to be his best man at the wedding! But when the ceremony was over, just as Liftsoff approached to congratulate the groom and kiss him as tradition dictates, he pulled out a knife and stabbed Golubenko instead! Can you believe it? The best man stabbed the groom! And then—this is the best part—the idiot ran around crying, 'Oh, what have I done? What have I done?' He hugged everyone in the room, including the ladies! Ha! They sent him to Siberia, where he starved to death. Poor Golubenko survived, though, if that makes you feel any better."

"I don't see why you're telling me this story," Velchaninoff said, frowning deeply.

"Well, because he stabbed the other guy with a knife," Pavel Pavlovitch replied with a mocking giggle. "It just shows that he wasn't some noble hero—he was just a fool who forgot the basic rules of behavior. Imagine clinging to women's necks like that, and in front of the governor, no less! Still, he did what he set out to do."

"Go to hell, you miserable liar!" shouted Velchaninoff, unable to contain his anger. His voice rose, and his chest heaved with rage. "You think you can scare me with your pathetic stories? You're nothing but a coward who frightens children! You're a disgusting, worthless scoundrel—yes, a scoundrel!"

Pavel Pavlovitch flinched as if struck. His drunkenness seemed to disappear in an instant. His lips trembled as he asked, "Are you calling me a scoundrel, Alexey Ivanovitch? Me?"

Velchaninoff paused, regaining his composure. "I'll apologize if you want," he said grimly, falling into a brooding silence. After a moment, he added, "But only if you agree to speak openly and honestly—right now."

"If I were you, I'd apologize unconditionally, Alexey Ivanovitch."

"Fine, so be it." Velchaninoff nodded. "I apologize. But admit it—you know I owe you nothing now. Not in this matter, or in anything else."

"Fair enough. What is there to settle between us?" Pavel Pavlovitch laughed without lifting his eyes.

"In that case, good. Now finish your wine and get to bed. You're not leaving tonight."

"Oh, the wine doesn't matter," muttered Pavel Pavlovitch as he picked up the tumbler. His hand trembled so much as he drank that some wine spilled on his waistcoat and the floor. Yet he drained the glass completely, as if he couldn't leave a drop behind. Placing the empty tumbler on the table, he shuffled to the bed, sat down, and began to undress.

"Maybe I shouldn't stay here tonight," he said suddenly, pausing with one boot off.

"I don't think so," Velchaninoff replied curtly, pacing the room and avoiding eye contact.

Pavel Pavlovitch finished undressing and lay down. A quarter-hour later, Velchaninoff also got into bed and extinguished the light.

Sleep did not come easily. A new unease gnawed at Velchaninoff, filling him with a mix of irritation and shame for letting it bother him. Just as he began to drift off, a faint rustling sound jolted him awake. He opened his eyes and glanced toward Pavel Pavlovitch's bed. Though the room was dark, it seemed as though Pavel Pavlovitch was no longer lying down but sitting on the edge of the bed.

"What's wrong?" Velchaninoff called out.

"A ghost," said Pavel Pavlovitch in a low voice after a few moments of silence.

"What? What kind of ghost?"

"Th-there, in that room, right at the door—I think I saw a ghost!"

"Whose ghost?" Velchaninoff paused before asking the question.

"Natalia Vasilievna's!"

Velchaninoff jumped out of bed and walked to the door, peering into the room across the passage. It had no curtains, so it was lighter than his own.

"There's nothing there at all. You're drunk—go back to bed!" he said, wrapping himself back in his blanket as he lay down.

Pavel Pavlovitch didn't reply but obediently lay down.

"Have you ever seen a ghost before?" Velchaninoff asked suddenly, about ten minutes later.

97

"I think I might have, once," Pavel Pavlovitch answered in the same low voice. Then silence fell again.

Velchaninoff wasn't sure if he'd fallen asleep or not, but about an hour later, he was suddenly wide awake. Had he heard a rustle? He couldn't tell. But something was clear now—there was something white standing in the middle of the dark room. It wasn't close to him, but it was there, unmistakable. He sat up in bed, staring at the figure for what felt like an eternity.

"Is that you, Pavel Pavlovitch?" he asked weakly. His voice sounded faint and uncertain.

There was no reply. Yet the figure didn't disappear—it was definitely still there.

"Is that you, Pavel Pavlovitch?" he shouted, louder this time, so loud that if Pavel Pavlovitch were still in bed, he would surely have woken and answered. But there was no response. The white figure seemed to be moving closer to him.

Something snapped inside Velchaninoff. He suddenly began shouting at the top of his voice, wild and furious, struggling to get his words out between gasps. "If you—drunken idiot that you are—think you can scare me, I'll show you how little I care! I'll turn my back to you, face the wall, and not look at you once the whole night! Stand there until morning if you want—I despise you!" With that, he twisted himself around, pulling the blanket tightly over him and pressing his face to the wall, lying as still as a statue.

The room fell into an eerie silence. He couldn't tell if the figure was still standing there or if it had moved. His heart pounded loudly in his chest. Minutes passed, and then, just a few steps from his bed, Pavel Pavlovitch's timid voice broke the silence.

"I got up, Alexey Ivanovitch, to look for some water. I couldn't find any and was just about to check near your bed…"

"Then why didn't you answer me when I called?" Velchaninoff asked angrily after a brief pause.

"I was scared. You shouted so loudly—you frightened me!"

"There's a carafe and glass on the little table over there. Light a candle if you need to."

"Oh, I'll find it in the dark. Please forgive me, Alexey Ivanovitch, for startling you. I got so thirsty all of a sudden."

Velchaninoff didn't respond. He kept his face turned toward the wall, lying perfectly still for the rest of the night. Whether it was out of stubbornness to prove his contempt for Pavel Pavlovitch or something else, he didn't know. His nerves were on edge, and sleep eluded him for a long time. He felt almost delirious, but eventually, he drifted off.

When he woke up past nine the next morning, he sat bolt upright in bed, startled as if someone had shaken him awake. Pavel Pavlovitch was gone. His bed was empty and rumpled—he had left before dawn.

"I knew it!" Velchaninoff exclaimed, smacking his forehead with the palm of his hand.

Chapter 10

The doctor's concern was well-founded. Liza's condition worsened significantly, far more than Velchaninoff and Claudia Petrovna had expected just the day before.

When Velchaninoff arrived in the morning, Liza was still conscious but burning with fever. Later, he told Claudia Petrovna that the child had smiled at him and held out her little hot hand. Whether this truly happened or was a projection of his desperate hope is uncertain.

By evening, however, Liza had slipped into unconsciousness, and she remained that way throughout her illness. Ten days after being moved to the countryside, she passed away.

This period was deeply sorrowful for Velchaninoff, and the Pogoryeltseffs were genuinely worried about him. He spent most of his time at their home, and during Liza's final days, he often sat alone for hours in a corner, lost in thought. Claudia Petrovna tried to distract him with conversation, but he would only respond briefly, if at all. It was clear that talking was painful for him, and Claudia was surprised by the depth of his grief.

The Pogoryeltseff children became his only source of comfort. With them, he could sometimes smile and even play, finding brief moments of relief. Yet, almost every hour, he would get up quietly and tiptoe to the sickroom to check on Liza. Occasionally, he imagined that she recognized him, though there was no hope left for her recovery— none of them held any hope. Still, he stayed close to her room, often sitting in the adjoining chamber.

Twice during this time, Velchaninoff acted with sudden urgency. He rushed into town, seeking out the best doctors and organizing consultations. The final consultation occurred the day before Liza's death.

A few days earlier, Claudia Petrovna had spoken to him firmly about the necessity of locating Pavel Pavlovitch. Without certain documents from him, Liza could not be buried properly if the worst were to happen. Velchaninoff agreed to write to him and managed to pen a brief note, which he delivered to the Pokrofsky. Pavel Pavlovitch was not at home, as usual, so Velchaninoff left the letter with Maria Sisevna.

Liza passed away on a beautiful summer evening as the sun was setting. Only then did Velchaninoff seem to come out of his daze.

When the little girl was laid out, adorned with flowers and dressed in a white frock borrowed from one of Claudia Petrovna's daughters, Velchaninoff approached Claudia with a fiery determination in his eyes. He declared that he would go and bring back the murderer. Ignoring all advice to wait until the next day, he set out for town immediately.

He already knew where to look for Pavel Pavlovitch. Over the past two days, Velchaninoff had not only gone to town to consult doctors. While watching over Liza in her final hours, he had been consumed by the idea that if he could find and bring Pavel Pavlovitch to her bedside, perhaps his voice might reach her and pull her back from the brink. In those desperate moments, he had twice rushed to town, driven by this fragile hope.

Pavel Pavlovitch's lodgings remained unchanged, but Velchaninoff knew it would be futile to search for him there. According to Maria Sisevna, Pavel Pavlovitch often disappeared for days at a time and was now frequently found among friends in the Voznecensky district.

When Velchaninoff arrived in town around ten o'clock, he went directly to the people he believed could help him locate Pavel Pavlovitch. Enlisting the assistance of one of them, he began his search.

He had no clear plan of what to do when he found Pavel Pavlovitch. Should he confront him violently, even kill him, or simply inform him of Liza's death and insist on his help with the funeral arrangements?

After a long and fruitless search, Velchaninoff stumbled upon Pavel Pavlovitch by chance. He found him in the street, in the middle of a drunken quarrel with another man over money. Pavel Pavlovitch seemed to be losing the argument. As soon as he spotted Velchaninoff, he stretched out his arms and pleaded for help. The other man, noticing Velchaninoff's imposing build, quickly retreated. Pavel Pavlovitch triumphantly shook his fist at the man and shouted after him, but his victory was short-lived.

Velchaninoff, driven by an emotion he couldn't fully understand, grabbed Pavel Pavlovitch by the shoulders and shook him violently. The drunkard's teeth chattered as Velchaninoff shook him harder and harder. Finally, exhausted, Velchaninoff released him, causing Pavel Pavlovitch to fall backward onto the pavement.

"Liza is dead!" Velchaninoff said sharply.

Pavel Pavlovitch sat there, staring blankly, his drunken mind struggling to process the words. For a moment, he seemed completely oblivious to what had been said. Finally, he whispered, "Dead," in an odd, almost indescribable tone. Velchaninoff couldn't tell whether Pavel Pavlovitch's face was twitching from emotion or whether he was attempting to grin in his usual unsettling way. Then, suddenly, Pavel Pavlovitch crossed himself with a trembling hand. He struggled to his feet and staggered away, seeming to forget Velchaninoff's presence entirely.

Velchaninoff quickly caught up to him and grabbed his shoulder again.

"Do you understand, you drunken fool, that the funeral can't happen without you?" Velchaninoff shouted, his rage boiling over.

Pavel Pavlovitch turned his head slightly. "The artillery lieutenant...
you remember him?" he muttered thickly.

"What?" Velchaninoff demanded, recoiling.

"He's her father... go find him. He'll bury her!" Pavel Pavlovitch
slurred.

"You liar!" Velchaninoff roared. "You're just saying that to be
spiteful. I knew you'd try to make up something like this!"

Overcome with fury, Velchaninoff struck Pavel Pavlovitch on the
head with his fist, putting all his strength into the blow. For a moment,
it seemed as though Velchaninoff might hit him again and kill him on
the spot. But Pavel Pavlovitch didn't flinch. Instead, he turned to
Velchaninoff, his face contorted with an expression of insane rage.

"Do you understand Russian?" he asked, his voice steadier now, as
though his anger had sobered him. "Then listen: you're a..." Pavel
Pavlovitch hurled an obscene insult, one of the foulest that could be
spoken in Russian. "Now, go back to her!" he shouted.

With that, Pavel Pavlovitch wrenched himself free from
Velchaninoff's grasp, nearly losing his balance in the process, and
staggered off down the street. Velchaninoff didn't follow him.

The next day, however, a respectable-looking middle-aged man in
a civil uniform arrived at the Pogoryeltseffs' house. He handed Claudia
Petrovna a packet, neatly addressed to her, with the sender listed as
"Pavel Pavlovitch Trusotsky."

The packet contained three hundred roubles along with all the
necessary documents for Liza's funeral. There was also a short note
from Pavel Pavlovitch, written with polite and formal language. He
sincerely thanked Claudia Petrovna for her great kindness to the
orphan, saying that only heaven could truly reward her. He explained,
in a somewhat confused manner, that severe illness prevented him

from attending the funeral of his "beloved and unfortunate daughter." However, he expressed full trust in Claudia Petrovna's "angelic goodness" to ensure that the ceremony would be carried out appropriately. The three hundred roubles, he noted, were to cover funeral costs and other expenses. Any leftover money, he requested, should be spent on prayers for Liza's soul.

The messenger who delivered the packet knew little about the matter. He explained that he had only agreed to act as the courier after Pavel Pavlovitch made an urgent appeal to him.

Pogoryeltseff was slightly offended by the offer of money to cover the expenses and considered returning it. However, Claudia Petrovna suggested obtaining a receipt from the cemetery authorities for the funeral costs, along with a statement that any remaining funds would be used for prayers as requested. Velchaninoff later mailed an envelope containing these documents to Pavel Pavlovitch's address.

After the funeral, Velchaninoff disappeared from the countryside entirely. For two weeks, he wandered aimlessly around town, bumping into people as he walked without purpose. Occasionally, he spent entire days lying in bed, ignoring basic needs and responsibilities. The Pogoryeltseffs repeatedly invited him to visit their home, and although he always promised to come, he inevitably forgot. Claudia Petrovna even came to his house to fetch him herself, but she found him absent. His lawyer, who had good news to share, faced similar difficulties. The legal dispute had been settled favorably for Velchaninoff, with his opponent accepting a modest settlement and relinquishing all claims to the contested property. The only thing left was for Velchaninoff to formally approve the agreement.

When the lawyer finally managed to find him at home after many attempts, he was shocked by Velchaninoff's indifference. Once fervently engaged in the matter, Velchaninoff now seemed entirely uninterested in the outcome.

By now, the hottest days of July had arrived, but Velchaninoff paid no attention to his surroundings. His grief consumed him, like a painful wound deep in his heart. His greatest regret was that Liza had died without ever truly knowing how much he loved her. The hope and light she had briefly brought into his life had been extinguished, leaving him in darkness once more.

He told himself, again and again, that his entire purpose in life should have been to surround Liza with love every day, every hour, and every moment. "No goal in life could be higher or more sacred than this," he thought in a mixture of despair and passion. "Even if other goals exist, none could be purer or more meaningful. My love for Liza should have cleansed and redeemed my flawed, wasted life. Instead of leaving behind my own sinful existence, I could have given the world a beautiful, innocent soul. Through her, I could have found forgiveness for myself."

These thoughts haunted Velchaninoff as he mourned the little girl. He reflected on every moment he had spent with her. He remembered her fevered face and how peaceful she had looked in her coffin, surrounded by flowers. One memory, in particular, tormented him: he had once noticed that one of her fingers was bruised and darkened, likely from a pinch or an injury. The sight of that little finger had ignited in him an overwhelming desire to confront and kill Pavel Pavlovitch.

The packet contained three hundred roubles, along with all the necessary documents for arranging Liza's funeral. Pavel Pavlovitch had written a short, polite note, expressing his deep gratitude to Claudia Petrovna for her great kindness towards the orphan. He wrote that such kindness could only be rewarded by heaven itself. In the note, he explained, somewhat unclearly, that he was unable to attend the funeral of his "beloved and unfortunate daughter" due to severe illness. He added that he had full confidence in Claudia Petrovna's "angelic goodness" to ensure that the ceremony would be conducted properly. The three hundred roubles, he stated, were intended to cover funeral and related expenses. Any remaining money, he requested, should be spent on prayers for Liza's soul.

The messenger who delivered the packet had little to add. He explained that he had only agreed to deliver it after Pavel Pavlovitch's urgent request and knew nothing more about the matter.

Pogoryeltseff felt somewhat offended by the offer of money for expenses and initially wanted to return it. However, Claudia Petrovna suggested that they accept it, as it was a father's duty to contribute to his child's burial. She recommended obtaining a receipt from the cemetery authorities for the funeral costs and a written statement confirming that the remaining funds would be used for prayers as requested. Velchaninoff later sent these documents to Pavel Pavlovitch's lodgings.

After the funeral, Velchaninoff disappeared from the countryside entirely. For two weeks, he wandered aimlessly around the city, bumping into people as he moved through the streets in a daze. At times, he spent entire days lying in bed, ignoring even the simplest tasks or needs. The Pogoryeltseffs frequently invited him to their home, and though he promised to visit, he always forgot. On one occasion, Claudia Petrovna went to fetch him herself but found him absent. His lawyer, who had good news to share, faced similar difficulties. The legal case had been resolved in Velchaninoff's favor, with his opponent accepting a small settlement and relinquishing all claims to the disputed property. All that was required was Velchaninoff's formal approval.

When the lawyer finally managed to find Velchaninoff at home, he was surprised by his indifference. Once deeply invested in the case, Velchaninoff now showed no interest in the outcome.

By this time, the hottest days of July had arrived, but Velchaninoff barely noticed. Grief consumed him, swelling in his chest like an unbearable weight. His greatest regret was that Liza had died before truly knowing him or realizing how deeply he loved her. The brief joy she had brought into his life—a light that had given him new purpose—was extinguished, leaving him in darkness once more.

As he reflected, Velchaninoff became convinced that his entire purpose in life should have been to surround Liza with love, every day, every hour, and every moment.

"There is no greater goal in life than this," he thought with sorrowful intensity. "If other purposes exist, none could be holier or more meaningful than this one. My flawed, wasted life could have been redeemed by my love for Liza. Through her, I could have left something pure and beautiful in this world—a part of me that would cleanse my guilt and offer me forgiveness. In her innocence, I could have forgiven myself."

These thoughts haunted him as he mourned the child. He remembered every detail about her: her flushed, feverish face, and later, her peaceful appearance in the coffin, surrounded by beautiful flowers. One memory, in particular, tormented him—a moment when he noticed one of her small fingers, bruised and blackened. He didn't know what had caused the injury, but the sight of it had ignited a burning desire to confront Pavel Pavlovitch and kill him on the spot.

Velchaninoff remembered something Pavel had once said to him: "Do you know what Liza is to me?" At the time, he hadn't fully understood, but now the meaning became clear. It wasn't an act or some show of affection—it was genuine love. But then, how could

Pavel have been so cruel to a child he loved so deeply? The thought was unbearable, and no answer seemed possible.

One day, without really knowing why, Velchaninoff found himself walking to the cemetery where Liza was buried. He searched until he found her grave. It was the first time he had been there since the funeral; he had avoided visiting, fearing it would be too painful. But to his surprise, kneeling down and kissing the small mound brought him a sense of peace and lightness he hadn't felt in a long time.

The evening was beautiful. The setting sun bathed everything in warm light, the tall grass around the graves swayed gently in the breeze, and a bee buzzed somewhere nearby. The flowers and crosses Claudia Petrovna had placed on Liza's grave were still there, undisturbed. For the first time in many days, Velchaninoff felt a flicker of hope in his heart.

"How light my heart feels," he thought as he absorbed the calmness of the cemetery and the stillness of the evening. A wave of faith—indescribable but real—filled his heart.

"This must be Liza's gift," he thought. "This is her speaking to me."

It was completely dark by the time he left the cemetery and began walking home.

Near the cemetery gates stood a small inn, its windows open to the warm night air. Velchaninoff glanced inside and noticed people sitting at tables. Then, to his astonishment, he spotted Pavel Pavlovitch among them, seated near a window. It was clear that Pavel had noticed him as well, watching him closely.

Velchaninoff continued walking, but before long, he heard hurried footsteps behind him. Of course, it was Pavel Pavlovitch. Perhaps the calm and peaceful expression on Velchaninoff's face as he had passed by had drawn him in, giving him the courage to approach.

Pavel quickly caught up and offered a timid smile—one that lacked the drunken smirk Velchaninoff had grown used to. In fact, he didn't seem drunk at all.

"Good evening," Pavel Pavlovitch said softly.

"How are you?" Velchaninoff replied.

Chapter 11

Velchaninoff surprised himself by answering Pavel Pavlovitch's greeting so calmly. It felt strange that he could meet this man now without any trace of anger. Instead, he felt something new—almost a sense of openness, as though their relationship might change.

"What a beautiful evening," said Pavel Pavlovitch, watching him closely.

"So, you haven't left yet," murmured Velchaninoff, not really asking, but more reflecting on the fact as he kept walking.

"I've been delayed, but I've finally got my petition approved—my new post, with a raise. I'm leaving the day after tomorrow, for sure."

"What? You've secured the new position?"

"And why wouldn't I?" Pavel Pavlovitch responded with a crooked smile.

"Oh, I didn't mean anything by it," Velchaninoff replied, frowning and giving him a sideways glance. To his surprise, Pavel Pavlovitch looked far more put-together than he had just a couple of weeks ago. Even his crape-banded hat was neat and tidy.

"Why was he sitting in the public house then?" Velchaninoff wondered. This contradiction baffled him.

"I wanted to share another bit of joyful news with you, Alexey Ivanovitch," Pavel said, breaking the silence.

"Joyful news?"

"I'm getting married."

"What?" Velchaninoff stopped and stared at him.

"Yes, sir! After sorrow comes joy—it's the way of life. Oh, Alexey Ivanovitch, I'd so much like—" Pavel began but hesitated. "But you seem to be in a hurry."

"Yes, I am. I'm not feeling well either." Velchaninoff's earlier willingness to consider a better relationship with Pavel had vanished completely. Now he just wanted to be rid of him.

"I'd so much like—" Pavel Pavlovitch tried again but trailed off. Velchaninoff said nothing, waiting for him to finish.

"In that case, perhaps another time—if we happen to meet again."

"Yes, yes, another time," Velchaninoff said quickly, picking up his pace and avoiding eye contact.

They walked in silence for a couple more minutes, with Pavel Pavlovitch still trailing beside him.

"Well then, goodbye for now," Pavel finally said. "Goodbye! I hope—"

Velchaninoff didn't wait to hear him finish. He turned and left, deeply unsettled. The encounter with Pavel had been too much for his fragile state of mind. As he lay down on his bed, one thought kept troubling him: "Why was that man near the cemetery?"

The next morning, Velchaninoff decided he would visit the Pogoryeltseffs. He didn't particularly want to go—he found any form of sympathy unbearable—but they had been so kind and concerned about him that he felt he owed it to them.

But while finishing his breakfast, he felt an overwhelming reluctance. The thought of facing them for the first time since his grief was daunting. "Should I go or not?" he wondered, sitting at the table, lost in thought.

Suddenly, to his shock and amazement, Pavel Pavlovitch walked into the room.

Velchaninoff could hardly believe his eyes. After their encounter the previous day, it seemed impossible that Pavel Pavlovitch would dare to enter his home again. Yet here he was. Velchaninoff was so stunned that he didn't know how to react. Pavel Pavlovitch, however, took control of the situation. He greeted him with a polite "Good morning," and sat down in the exact same chair he had used three weeks ago during his last visit.

The sight brought back unpleasant memories of that earlier meeting, and Velchaninoff glared at his visitor with a mixture of disgust and unease.

"I can see that you're surprised!" Pavel Pavlovitch said, reading his expression.

This time, Pavel seemed both more relaxed and yet more nervous than the day before. His appearance was strikingly different—he wasn't just dressed neatly; he was dressed to impress. He wore a stylish summer overcoat, light trousers, and a crisp white waistcoat. His gloves, gold-rimmed glasses (a new addition), and his freshly laundered linen all looked impeccable. Even a faint scent of perfume lingered in the air around him. He looked almost comical, but his polished appearance also gave Velchaninoff a strange, uneasy feeling.

"Of course, my appearance has surprised you, Alexey Ivanovitch," Pavel said, fidgeting in his seat. "I can see it in your face. But don't you think there should be something higher, something beyond petty disagreements and the everyday concerns of life that connects one man to another? Don't you agree?"

"Pavel Pavlovitch," Velchaninoff interrupted sharply, his frown deepening, "get to the point. Say what you have to say quickly and stop wasting my time."

"I'll be brief," Pavel said hastily. "I'm getting married, and I'm leaving shortly to visit my bride in the countryside. What I'm here to ask, Alexey Ivanovitch, is the great honor of your company. I want to introduce you to her family, sir. That's why I've come—to ask you to accompany me." Pavel bowed his head respectfully as he spoke.

"You want me to go with you? To where?" Velchaninoff asked, his astonishment plain as his eyes widened.

"To their house in the countryside," Pavel clarified. "Forgive me if I seem nervous or if my words are jumbled, but I'm terribly afraid you'll refuse me."

He looked at Velchaninoff with a pleading expression.

"You want me to meet your bride?" Velchaninoff asked, staring at him, unable to believe what he was hearing.

"Yes, that's exactly it," Pavel replied in a soft, timid voice. "Don't be angry with me, Alexey Ivanovitch. This isn't some act of arrogance on my part. I ask with all humility, fully aware of how unusual my request is. I—I just hoped you wouldn't say no."

"First of all, it's completely out of the question," Velchaninoff replied, turning away as a wave of confusion swept over him.

"I'm only asking because I have a very important reason," Pavel said earnestly. "I'll explain everything to you later, I promise. But for now, I—"

"No matter what your reason is, it's impossible!" Velchaninoff interrupted, his frustration rising. "Even you must see that!"

"Not at all, sir. It's entirely possible," Pavel argued. "First, I'll introduce you simply as my friend. And second, you already know the family—the Zachlebnikoffs. State Councillor Zachlebnikoff!"

Velchaninoff was startled. "What? How's that possible?" he exclaimed. This was the very man he had spent so much time trying to track down—the lawyer who had represented his opponent in the recent legal case.

"Yes, that's right!" Pavel Pavlovitch replied, gaining confidence at Velchaninoff's astonishment. "He's the same man I saw you speaking to in the street one day. I was watching you from across the road, waiting for my turn to talk to him. We worked in the same department about twelve years ago. But I swear, at that time, I had no idea any of this would happen. The idea only came to me a week ago."

"Wait a second—surely this is a very respectable family, isn't it?" Velchaninoff asked naively.

"Well, what if it is respectable?" Pavel answered with a smirk.

"No, I didn't mean anything by it," Velchaninoff replied quickly. "But, from what little I saw—"

"They remember your visit!" Pavel interrupted, clearly delighted. "I told them all kinds of flattering things about you."

"But how can you even think about marrying just three months after your wife passed away?" Velchaninoff asked.

"Oh, the wedding doesn't have to be right away. We can wait nine or ten months so that I'll have been in mourning for a full year. Believe me, everything about this arrangement is ideal. Fedosie Petrovitch has known me since I was a boy. He knew my late wife, knows my financial situation, my private savings, and now my increased salary. It's all just a matter of balancing the scales."

"Is the bride one of his daughters?"

"Yes," Pavel replied, licking his lips as if savoring the thought. "May I smoke a cigarette? Now, imagine this: a man like Fedosie

114

Petrovitch is highly valued by the State. But his pay is pitiful—barely enough to live on, aside from a few perks. He's got eight daughters and only one little boy. If he dies, all they'll have is a small pension to scrape by on. Can you even imagine the expense of just buying shoes for a family like that? Five of the daughters are already of marriageable age— the eldest is twenty-four, and she's absolutely stunning. You'll see her yourself if you come. The sixth is still in school, only fifteen. All those girls need to be married off, and that takes money. Then I appear on the scene, the first eligible suitor they've had, and they know I have money. Well, there you go—it's all settled."

Pavel was clearly thrilled with himself.

"Are you engaged to the eldest?" Velchaninoff asked.

"No, not the eldest. I'm pursuing the sixth girl, the one still in school."

"What?" Velchaninoff laughed, unable to help himself. "You just said she's only fifteen!"

"She's fifteen now," Pavel replied calmly, "but she'll be sixteen in nine months—sixteen and three months. Why not? Of course, we won't announce the engagement publicly just yet. It's still a private arrangement between her parents and me. But believe me, everything about this is perfect and proper."

"So it's not finalized yet?"

"Oh, it's completely finalized! As good as done."

"Does she even know about it?"

"Well, officially, no one's said anything to her yet—it's just for appearances. But she knows. She definitely knows. Oh, Alexey Ivanovitch, please agree to come with me!" he pleaded, his voice filled with desperation.

"But why should I go with you?" Velchaninoff asked, growing impatient. "Actually, since I have no intention of going, there's no point in listening to your reasons."

"Alexey Ivanovitch—"

"Oh, come on! Do you really think I'm going to sit in a carriage next to you and ride down there? Be serious!" Velchaninoff snapped. "Think about what you're asking."

The initial amusement Pavel's ridiculous talk had sparked was now replaced by disgust and anger. Velchaninoff felt his irritation rising with every moment. He could hardly bear the thought of being near this man and feared that, if the conversation went on any longer, he might lose control and throw him out of the house. For some reason, he was furious with himself as well.

Pavel Pavlovitch spoke in a pleading tone. "Please, Alexey Ivanovitch, sit down! You won't regret it, I promise you!" He quickly added, as Velchaninoff made an impatient gesture, "No, no, hear me out. I beg you to think carefully before giving me your final answer. I believe you've misunderstood my intentions. I know very well that we are not alike, and that I cannot expect to fit into your life. I'm not blind to that fact. What I'm asking of you now won't bind you to me in any way in the future. I'm leaving the day after tomorrow, without fail. Let this one day be an exception for me. I came to you hoping to appeal to the kindness and nobility of your heart, Alexey Ivanovitch—to the softer feelings that recent events may have awakened in you. Am I making myself clear, or do you still misunderstand me?"

Pavel Pavlovitch grew increasingly agitated as he spoke.

Velchaninoff watched him closely.

"You're asking something from me," he said thoughtfully, "and you're pressing me quite hard about it. That makes me suspicious. I need to know more."

"All I'm asking is for you to come with me. I swear, when we return, I'll open my heart to you as if you were my confessor. Just trust me this one time, Alexey Ivanovitch!"

But Velchaninoff hesitated. He resisted more firmly because he felt a strange, nagging sensation ever since Pavel had begun speaking about his bride. He couldn't tell if it was pure curiosity or something deeper, but whatever it was, it made him feel uneasy. The more this feeling urged him to agree, the more he dug in his heels.

He sat for a long time, resting his head on his hand, while Pavel Pavlovitch hovered around, continuing to argue his case.

Finally, Velchaninoff said, "Fine, I'll go." His voice shook slightly as he spoke. Pavel Pavlovitch beamed with joy.

"Excellent, Alexey Ivanovitch! Now, go and change. Dress up in your usual elegant way—you do it so well."

As Velchaninoff dressed, Pavel flitted around him, nearly giddy with happiness.

"What is this man up to?" Velchaninoff wondered.

"Just one more favor, Alexey Ivanovitch," Pavel said suddenly. "You'll be my guide too."

"What do you mean by that?"

"Well, for instance, this matter of the crape band on my hat. Should I remove it or leave it on?"

"That's entirely up to you."

"No, I want your opinion. What would you do in my position? I thought leaving it on would show my loyalty and affection. A nice touch, wouldn't you say?"

"Take it off, of course."

"Do you really think so?" Pavel reflected for a moment. "No, I think I'll leave it on."

"Do as you please," Velchaninoff muttered to himself. "At least he doesn't trust me, which is a small comfort."

Finally, they left the house. Pavel examined Velchaninoff's sharp attire with obvious satisfaction. Velchaninoff was puzzled by Pavel's behavior but equally baffled by his own willingness to go along with it. At the gate, an elegant open carriage waited for them.

"So, you had a carriage ready," Velchaninoff remarked dryly. "You were confident I'd agree to come with you?"

"I arranged the carriage for myself, but I was pretty sure you'd come," Pavel said, his voice full of contentment.

"You have a lot of faith in my generosity," Velchaninoff said as they climbed into the carriage. Though he smiled, his heart brimmed with irritation.

"Well, Alexey Ivanovitch, surely you can't call me a fool for having faith in you," Pavel replied firmly, his tone unexpectedly serious.

As the carriage rolled along, Velchaninoff's thoughts turned briefly to Liza. He quickly pushed them away, feeling it was inappropriate to think of her here. Almost immediately, he felt ashamed. How small and petty he must be, he thought, to associate such trivial sentiments with Liza's sacred memory. The thought angered him so much that he almost ordered the carriage to stop, ready to jump out even if it meant arguing with Pavel Pavlovitch.

Just then, Pavel broke the silence, pulling Velchaninoff back into the present. "Alexey Ivanovitch," he said, "are you good at judging valuable items?"

"What kind of items?" Velchaninoff asked.

"Diamonds."

"Yes."

"I want to buy a gift to take with me. What do you think? Should I give her one or not?"

"I don't think it's necessary."

"But I really want to. The only question is, what should I get? A full set—brooch, earrings, bracelet, and everything—or just one piece?"

"How much are you planning to spend?"

"Oh, four or five hundred roubles."

"Ridiculous!"

"What? Too much?"

"Buy one bracelet for about a hundred."

Pavel Pavlovitch looked deflated. He had been eager to spend a lot of money and buy an entire set. He kept insisting it was necessary.

When they reached a shop, Pavel ended up buying a bracelet, but not the one he wanted. He bought the one Velchaninoff picked. Pavel had wanted to buy both, and when the shopkeeper lowered the price from one hundred seventy-five to one hundred fifty roubles, Pavel wasn't pleased. He would have happily paid two hundred if anyone had encouraged him.

Once they were back in the carriage and on their way again, Pavel grew excited. "It's all right, isn't it, to give her a gift so soon?" he asked nervously. "They're not fancy people at all. They live very simply.

Innocence appreciates presents," he added with a sly smile. "You laughed earlier, Alexey Ivanovitch, when I said she was only fifteen. But you know what struck me most about her? She still goes to school with a little bag in her hand, full of copybooks and pencils. Ha-ha-ha! That little satchel got to me. I love innocence, Alexey Ivanovitch. Good looks don't matter to me half as much as innocence. Just imagine, the other day she and her friend were sitting in a corner laughing so hard because a cat jumped off a cupboard, landed on the sofa, and tumbled off. That kind of laughter smells like fresh apples, doesn't it? Should I take off the crape, do you think?"

"Do whatever you like," Velchaninoff replied.

"All right, I'll take it off!" Pavel pulled off the crape band from his hat and threw it onto the road. When he put his hat back on, his face was lit up with a simple, childlike joy.

"Is this who he really is?" Velchaninoff wondered, annoyed. "Can he really be dragging me down here without some hidden motive? That's impossible! He can't just be relying on my generosity." The thought made him indignant. "What kind of man is this?" he continued to ponder. "Is he a fool, an idiot, or just some hopeless 'permanent husband'? I can't make any sense of it!"

Chapter 12

The Zachlebnikoff family was, as Velchaninoff had described them, extremely respectable. Mr. Zachlebnikoff himself was a man of impressive dignity and authority, with a solid and reliable air about him. However, Pavel Pavlovitch's comment about their financial situation was entirely accurate—they lived comfortably, but if the head of the family were to pass away, the rest would face significant difficulties.

Mr. Zachlebnikoff greeted Velchaninoff warmly and with great courtesy. This time, he was not an opposing party in a legal battle but instead came across as a congenial and pleasant host.

"Congratulations," he said right away. "On the settlement, of course. I worked to ensure it ended this way, and your lawyer was a fine man to work with. Now you've secured your sixty thousand without any unnecessary hassle. If we hadn't settled, the case might have dragged on for years."

Velchaninoff was introduced to Mrs. Zachlebnikoff as well, a modest and slightly worn-looking older woman. Afterward, the daughters began appearing, some one by one and others in pairs. To Velchaninoff's surprise, there seemed to be far more girls than he had been led to expect. Soon, ten or even a dozen young women were gathered, and he realized that some were friends from neighboring homes.

The Zachlebnikoffs' country house was a large wooden structure, not particularly stylish in design but still quite attractive. It had a spacious garden, though the grounds were shared with two or three other nearby houses. This arrangement had fostered a close bond between the Zachlebnikoff daughters and the young ladies from the neighboring families.

Velchaninoff quickly noticed that his visit—accompanying Pavel Pavlovitch as a friend and being introduced to the family—had been anticipated as a significant and formal event.

As someone skilled in reading social cues, he soon realized there was even more to their reception. The parents were exceptionally polite, and the young women were dressed with unusual care. Velchaninoff suspected that Pavel Pavlovitch had made the most of the situation, likely hinting—though not outright saying—that Velchaninoff was a wealthy bachelor, lonely and perhaps ready to settle down, especially after recently inheriting a considerable fortune.

Katerina Fedosievna, the eldest daughter at twenty-four, stood out among her siblings. According to Pavel, she was a "splendid girl," and her elegant outfit and intricately styled hair seemed designed to make an impression. Velchaninoff guessed that much of the family's attention was focused on presenting Katerina as a potential match for him.

The other sisters also seemed to understand that Velchaninoff was there to meet Katerina. Their glances and comments subtly reinforced the idea, as though they were all playing their parts in an unspoken plan.

Katerina was a tall, attractive young woman, with a curvy figure and a calm, almost drowsy demeanor. Velchaninoff found her very pleasant to look at and thought it strange that such a fine young woman remained unmarried.

All the sisters were appealing in their way, and several of the visiting friends were quite pretty as well. The lively company of so many young women amused Velchaninoff greatly.

Nadejda Fedosievna, the schoolgirl who was Pavel Pavlovitch's intended bride, had not yet appeared. Velchaninoff found himself waiting for her arrival with a surprising degree of impatience that both amused and puzzled him. At last, she entered, making quite an impression. She was accompanied by a lively friend, Maria Nikitishna, a woman several years older than her. Maria was well known to the family, having served as a governess in a neighboring house for years. At twenty-three, she was highly regarded by the other girls and seemed to act as both mentor and confidante to Nadia.

From the moment Nadia entered, Velchaninoff noticed that all the girls, including Maria, seemed opposed to Pavel Pavlovitch. It didn't take him long to see that Nadia not only disliked but utterly despised him. What surprised him even more was that Pavel Pavlovitch either failed to notice this or chose to ignore it entirely.

Nadia was the most beautiful of all the girls. She was a petite brunette with a bold, spirited expression that hinted at rebellion. Her sharp, lively eyes sparkled mischievously, and her charming smile often carried a hint of defiance rather than friendliness. Her lips and teeth were stunning, and though she was slim, her figure was well-proportioned. Her face carried a thoughtful look, though it still retained the playfulness of youth.

Her age—just fifteen—was evident in every feature and movement. As Velchaninoff later learned, Pavel Pavlovitch had first noticed her on her way back from school, carrying a small satchel. Ever since that day, she had stopped using it.

The gift Pavel Pavlovitch brought with him turned out to be a disaster and left an awkward impression.

As soon as Nadia entered the room, Pavel Pavlovitch approached her with a wide, forced grin. Holding out the present, he stammered something about offering it in honor of the pleasant memory of her singing a certain song at the piano during his last visit. He then fell silent, fumbling as he pushed the jeweler's box into her hands. Nadia, however, refused to take it and pulled her hands away.

She turned to her mother, her tone commanding, and said loudly, "I won't take it, Mother." Her face flushed with both anger and embarrassment.

Her mother, clearly uncomfortable, didn't know how to respond, but her father stepped in with quiet authority. "Take it and thank Pavel Pavlovitch for it," he said firmly, though his displeasure was evident.

Muttering that it wasn't necessary, Pavel Pavlovitch tried to dismiss the moment, but the damage was already done. Nadia, realizing she had no choice, finally took the box. She gave a quick, mechanical curtsy, bobbing down and back up as though on springs, much like a child being scolded into politeness.

One of her sisters stepped forward to see the gift, and Nadia handed the box to her without even opening it, making it clear she couldn't care less about its contents.

The bracelet was taken out and passed around the room. Everyone examined it in silence, with a few casting skeptical or amused glances. Only the mother murmured half-heartedly that it was "very pretty."

Pavel Pavlovitch, meanwhile, looked as though he wished the floor would open up and swallow him whole.

Seeing his misery, Velchaninoff decided to rescue him from further humiliation. He suddenly began speaking loudly and animatedly about whatever came to mind. Within minutes, he had captured the attention of everyone in the room. Velchaninoff was a skilled conversationalist, particularly in social settings. He had a knack for sounding entirely genuine while giving the impression that he believed his listeners to be equally sincere.

He expertly played the role of a carefree, cheerful man, weaving occasional clever jokes into his speech. Though these jokes often seemed spontaneous, they were carefully prepared and sometimes even recycled from previous conversations. His effortless charm quickly eased the tension in the room.

Today, Velchaninoff was on top form. He felt confident that he could dominate the room, captivating everyone's attention with his words. He knew that soon, every laugh would be at his jokes, and every conversation would circle back to him.

As expected, his presence quickly transformed the atmosphere. Before long, the chatter and laughter grew lively, with Velchaninoff at the center of it all. Mrs. Zachlebnikoff's warm face lit up with genuine joy, and Katie's sparkling eyes betrayed her fascination. Her entire expression glowed with delight.

Only Nadia sat watching him with a frown, her sharp eyes peeking out from beneath her dark lashes. It was obvious she didn't like him, and her coldness only motivated Velchaninoff to put in even more effort. Meanwhile, mischievous Maria Nikitishna, clearly siding with Nadia, managed to tease him successfully. She jokingly claimed that Pavel Pavlovitch had described Velchaninoff as his childhood friend, making him out to be seven or eight years older than he really was. Despite the jest, Velchaninoff found himself liking Maria.

Pavel Pavlovitch, on the other hand, seemed utterly bewildered. At first, he appeared proud of Velchaninoff's success, laughing along with the jokes and joining the conversation. However, as time went on, his mood shifted. He grew quiet, slipping into deep thought and eventually into a visible melancholy, which was evident from his gloomy and tired expression.

"Well, my good man, you're the sort of guest who entertains himself," said old Zachlebnikoff cheerfully as he rose to leave for his

125

study. "And to think I was told you were the gloomiest of hypochondriacs! My, how wrong people can be about others!"

A grand piano stood in the room, and Velchaninoff suddenly turned to Nadia and asked, "You sing, don't you?"

"Who said that?" Nadia replied sharply.

"Pavel Pavlovitch told me."

"That's not true. I only sing for fun—I don't have a real voice."

"Oh, but I don't have a voice either, and yet I sing!" Velchaninoff said with a grin.

"Well, you go first, then I'll sing," Nadia said, her eyes gleaming. "Not now, though—after dinner. I hate music," she added. "I'm sick of the piano. It's nothing but singing and playing here all day. Katie's the only one of us who's worth listening to!"

Velchaninoff wasted no time turning his attention to Katie, showering her with requests to play. His focus on her eldest daughter made Mrs. Zachlebnikoff so pleased that her face flushed with pride.

Katie finally agreed, walking to the piano with her cheeks as red as a schoolgirl's. She was clearly embarrassed by her own reaction. She played a short piece by Haydn, performing it accurately but without much feeling.

When she finished, Velchaninoff enthusiastically praised both the piece and Haydn's music in general. His admiration wasn't limited to the music, though; the way he looked at Katie was unmistakable. His expression seemed to say, "My goodness, you're a stunning woman!" The message was so clear that everyone in the room picked up on it— especially Katie herself.

"What a lovely garden you have," said Velchaninoff after a brief pause, glancing out through the glass doors of the balcony. "Shall we all go outside?"

"Oh, yes! Let's go!" several voices chimed in at once. It seemed he had suggested exactly what everyone wanted.

They all headed into the garden and strolled around until it was time for dinner. Velchaninoff used the chance to get better acquainted with some of the girls. A few young men from the nearby houses joined them—a student, a schoolboy, and another young man of about twenty wearing large spectacles. Each of these newcomers quickly paired off with a young lady they seemed to favor.

The young man in spectacles immediately sought out Nadia and Maria Nikitishna. They stepped aside and began an animated conversation, speaking in low voices with intense expressions and lots of frowning.

This young man made no attempt to hide his disdain for Pavel Pavlovitch, treating him with outright contempt.

Some of the girls suggested playing a game. One proposed "Proverbs," but the idea was dismissed as dull. Another mentioned acting, but someone argued they never knew how to wrap things up properly.

"Maybe it will work better with you," Nadia said to Velchaninoff with a hint of confidence. "We all thought you were Pavel Pavlovitch's friend, but now it seems he was just bragging. I'm glad you came— really glad, for a certain reason!" She gave him a knowing look and then retreated back to Maria's side, blushing.

"We'll play 'Proverbs' this evening," another girl declared, "and we'll tease Pavel Pavlovitch. You'll help, won't you?"

"We're so glad you're here. It's usually so boring," added a third girl, a funny-looking redhead with a flushed face as if she'd been running. Velchaninoff had no idea where she had come from—he hadn't noticed her earlier.

Meanwhile, Pavel Pavlovitch's discomfort grew by the minute. Velchaninoff, however, used the opportunity to become friendly with Nadia. Her initial frowns had vanished, and now she was full of energy, dancing and jumping around, singing and whistling, and sometimes even grabbing his hand in a burst of playful cheerfulness.

She seemed delighted, completely ignoring Pavel Pavlovitch as though he weren't even there.

Pavel Pavlovitch, on the other hand, grew increasingly jealous. Whenever Nadia and Velchaninoff talked privately, he would barge in, shoving his face between them to interrupt.

By now, it was clear to Katia that the charming guest had not come for her as everyone had initially believed. Velchaninoff was clearly so interested in Nadia that he paid little attention to anyone else. Still, Katia's good-natured face showed no bitterness. She seemed content enough watching everyone else's happiness and listening to the lively chatter, even though she couldn't contribute much to the conversation herself.

"What a wonderful girl your sister Katerina Fedosievna is," Velchaninoff remarked to Nadia.

"Katia? Of course! There's no one better in the whole world. She's our family angel! Honestly, I'm in love with her myself!" Nadia replied with enthusiasm.

Finally, dinner was announced, and it was a splendid meal with several extra courses added for the guests. A bottle of tokay was brought out, and champagne was passed around to celebrate the occasion. Everyone was in high spirits, and even old Zachlebnikoff was unusually cheerful, having indulged in an extra glass of wine. The merriment was contagious, and even Pavel Pavlovitch worked up the courage to make a joke. From his seat at the far end of the table, next to the lady of the house, a burst of laughter erupted from the delighted girls who heard his first attempt at humor.

"Papa, papa, Pavel Pavlovitch made a joke!" several of the girls cried out at once. "He said there's a 'galaxy of gals' here!"

"A joke, did he? What is it? Let's hear it!" said the old man, his face lighting up as he turned toward Pavel Pavlovitch, ready to laugh even before understanding the joke.

"He says there's a 'galaxy of gals,' papa!" the girls explained.

"Well, where's the joke in that?" asked Zachlebnikoff, still failing to grasp it but smiling warmly with the desire to understand.

"Oh, papa, you're so slow! 'Gals' and 'galaxy'—don't you get it? He's saying there's a gal-axy of gals here!" the girls giggled.

"Oh! Oh!" laughed the old man, finally catching on. "Ha-ha! Well, let's hope he comes up with a better one next time!"

"Pavel Pavlovitch can't be expected to master everything at once," added Maria Nikitishna with a grin. "Oh, my goodness, look! He's swallowed a bone!" she suddenly exclaimed, jumping up from her chair.

The room was thrown into a brief panic, much to Maria's delight.

It turned out Pavel Pavlovitch had only choked on his wine, which he quickly drank to recover from his embarrassment. However, Maria insisted it was a fishbone and claimed she'd seen it with her own eyes, adding that people had been known to die from swallowing bones like that.

"Clap him on the back!" someone shouted.

Several eager hands rushed forward to help, despite Pavel's protests that it was just a harmless cough. The back-slapping continued until his coughing subsided, and it became clear that Maria had stirred up the commotion on purpose.

After dinner, old Mr. Zachlebnikoff retired for his customary nap, advising the young people to enjoy themselves in the garden.

"Make sure you have a good time, too!" he added, giving Pavel Pavlovitch an encouraging pat on the shoulder as he left.

Once the group had gathered in the garden again, Pavel Pavlovitch suddenly approached Velchaninoff and whispered urgently, "Just a moment," tugging at his sleeve.

The two men stepped aside into a quiet, secluded path.

"None of that here! I won't have it!" Pavel Pavlovitch hissed in a strained whisper.

"None of what? What are you talking about?" Velchaninoff asked, staring at him in bewilderment. Pavel Pavlovitch stayed silent, glaring at Velchaninoff, his lips twitching as he struggled to keep a fake smile. Suddenly, the voices of the girls calling them to join a game broke the tension. Velchaninoff shrugged and walked back to the group, with Pavel following behind.

"I bet Pavel Pavlovitch was asking to borrow a handkerchief again," teased Maria. "He forgot his handkerchief last time too, and of course, he has a cold as always!"

"Oh, Pavel Pavlovitch, why didn't you say so?" exclaimed Mrs. Zachlebnikoff, hurrying toward the house. "You'll have one right away."

Poor Pavel tried to explain that he had two handkerchiefs and wasn't suffering from a cold, but Mrs. Zachlebnikoff, eager for an excuse to leave, paid no attention. Moments later, a maid approached Pavel with a handkerchief, much to his embarrassment.

The group decided to play "Proverbs." Everyone sat down while the young man with glasses was sent to stand far away, nose against the wall, until the proverb was chosen and the words arranged. Velchaninoff's turn to be the questioner followed next.

Then it was Pavel Pavlovitch's turn. By this time, he had regained some of his good spirits and obediently took his place by the wall, determined to play properly. The red-haired girl was assigned to keep watch to ensure he didn't cheat.

As soon as Pavel had taken his spot, the entire group dashed off, running away as fast as they could.

"Run quickly!" whispered the girls to Velchaninoff, who hadn't moved.

"What's going on? What's the joke?" he asked, hurrying to catch up.

"Shh! Don't make a sound! We're leaving him there to stand all by himself—that's the joke."

Katia, however, didn't approve. When the last stragglers, including Velchaninoff, reached the end of the garden, they found her scolding the group angrily.

"Fine," she said, "I won't tell Mother this time, but I'm leaving. It's too cruel! How would you feel if you were left alone like that, standing there?"

With that, she stormed off. The rest of the group, however, found the prank hilarious and thoroughly enjoyed it. They begged Velchaninoff to act as though nothing had happened when Pavel returned.

It was a full fifteen minutes before Pavel showed up again, most of which he must have spent standing by the wall. When he finally rejoined them, he found the group laughing and shouting, completely engrossed in a lively game of Goriélki.

Seething with rage, Pavel made a beeline for Velchaninoff and yanked on his coat sleeve. "One moment, sir!"

"Oh no, he's back with his 'one moments!'" someone teased.

"Probably needs another handkerchief!" another voice chimed in as the two walked away.

"This time it was you!" Pavel muttered, his teeth chattering with anger. "You started this insult!"

Velchaninoff cut him off and firmly suggested he try to cheer up. "You're getting teased because you lose your temper," he said. "If you just lighten up and join in, they'll leave you alone."

Pavel Pavlovitch seemed genuinely affected by Velchaninoff's advice. He calmed down immediately and returned to the group looking ashamed. He even joined in the games with a renewed effort to enjoy himself. To everyone's surprise, no one teased him again, and within half an hour, he seemed to be in good spirits.

What surprised Velchaninoff even more was that Pavel didn't try to speak to Nadia, though he stayed as close to her as possible whenever he could. He accepted her obvious disdain without protest, as if it was perfectly normal.

Before the evening ended, however, Pavel became the target of another prank. During a game of hide-and-seek, he hid in a small room inside the house. Someone saw him go in, locked the door, and left him trapped there for an hour while he fumed in frustration.

Meanwhile, Velchaninoff learned the true reason for Nadia's excitement at his arrival. Maria led him to a quiet path in the garden where Nadia was waiting for him alone.

"I've figured out," Nadia began, once Maria left them, "that you aren't nearly as close to Pavel Pavlovitch as he pretended. I also believe that only you can help me with something very important." She pulled a small jewelry case out of her pocket. "Here's his horrible bracelet. I need you to return it to him for me. I can't do it myself because I've decided I'll never speak to him again, ever. You can tell him that for me. Also, tell him not to bother me with any more of his awful gifts. I'll send him the rest of what I need to say through someone else. Will you do this for me?"

"Oh, please, spare me!" Velchaninoff exclaimed, almost wringing his hands.

"Spare you?" Nadia asked, shocked. Her attempt at sounding composed crumbled instantly, and her eyes welled up as if she might cry. Velchaninoff couldn't help but laugh.

"I don't mean I won't—I'd be happy to—but the problem is, I have my own issues to deal with when it comes to him!"

"I knew it! You aren't really his friend, and he was lying all along. I will never marry him—never! You can count on that. I don't even understand how he dares—anyway, you have to return this awful bracelet. What will I do if you don't? He needs to get it back today. He'll regret it if he causes trouble with my father over me!"

Just then, the bespectacled young man emerged from the bushes nearby.

"You have a responsibility to return the bracelet," he declared angrily at Velchaninoff, "out of respect for women's rights—"

Before he could finish, Nadia grabbed his arm and pulled him away with all her strength. "How stupid can you be?" she yelled. "Go away! How dare you eavesdrop? I told you to stay far back!" She stamped her foot in fury. Even after he slunk off, she walked beside Velchaninoff, her eyes flashing with anger.

"You wouldn't believe how foolish he is!" she finally said. "You're laughing, but imagine how I feel!"

"That's not him, is it?" Velchaninoff teased, laughing.

"Of course not! How could you even think that? He's just a friend of his, but I don't understand how he picks such ridiculous friends. They call him a 'future leader,' but I don't see it. Alexey Ivanovitch, this is my last request—I have no one else to ask. Will you give the bracelet back or not?"

"All right, I will. Give it to me."

Nadia was overjoyed. "Oh, thank you, Alexey Ivanovitch! You're so kind!" she exclaimed with excitement. "For that, I'll sing all evening! I sing beautifully, you know! I was teasing you with a silly story before dinner. Oh, I wish you'd come here again—I'd tell you everything, and so much more besides. You're such a wonderful person—just like Katia!"

True to her word, when they returned to the house, Nadia sat at the piano and sang two songs. Her voice was completely untrained, but it was naturally sweet and surprisingly powerful.

When the group came back from the garden, they found Pavel Pavlovitch sitting on the balcony with the elder members of the family, drinking tea. He had likely been having a serious conversation, as he was preparing to leave in two days for nine months. He didn't even glance at Velchaninoff or the others when they arrived, but it was clear he hadn't complained to the family. For now, all was calm. However, as soon as Nadia began singing, he came into the room. She ignored every one of his questions, but Pavel didn't seem upset. Instead, he positioned himself behind her chair, as if claiming that spot was his rightful place.

"Now it's Alexey Ivanovitch's turn to sing!" the girls shouted after Nadia finished her songs, gathering eagerly around Velchaninoff as he sat down at the piano. He chose an old song by Glinka, which was rarely performed anymore. The words began:

"When from your merry lips

Tenderness flows..."

Velchaninoff sang with his eyes fixed on Nadia, almost as if the words were meant just for her. Though his voice was not what it once had been, it was clear that he had sung well in his youth. This song held a special place in his heart, as he had heard it sung years ago by Glinka himself during his university days. The passion in the music brought back vivid memories, and he delivered the song with heartfelt expression.

As soon as he finished, the room erupted in applause. But before Velchaninoff could bask in the admiration, Pavel Pavlovitch stormed forward. Seizing Nadia's hand, he pulled her away from Velchaninoff and then turned back to the piano. His face twisted with fury, and his trembling lips barely formed the words, "I need a word with you."

Velchaninoff, seeing Pavel's uncontrollable rage, decided not to provoke him further. Taking Pavel's hand, he led him through the balcony and out into the now-dark garden.

"You must leave immediately—this very moment!" Pavel hissed.

"No, I don't think so," Velchaninoff replied calmly.

"Do you remember," Pavel continued, his voice trembling with anger, "how you asked me to tell you everything? Every little detail? Well, the time has come for me to tell you—come with me now!"

Velchaninoff paused to consider Pavel's words. After a moment's thought, he glanced at him again and finally agreed.

"Oh, but stay and have another cup of tea!" Mrs. Zachlebnikoff called after them as they announced their departure.

"Why are you taking Alexey Ivanovitch away?" the girls demanded with annoyed expressions. Nadia glared at Pavel with such intensity that he squirmed uncomfortably under her gaze, but he didn't back down.

"Oh, I'm very grateful to Pavel Pavlovitch," Velchaninoff said with a laugh. "He's reminded me of some urgent business I might have forgotten otherwise." He shook hands with the host and gave a polite bow to the ladies, especially Katia, as the family believed he was most interested in her.

"You must come back soon!" said Mr. Zachlebnikoff warmly. "We've so enjoyed your visit!"

"Yes, please come again!" added his wife.

"Do come back, Alexey Ivanovitch!" called the girls as Pavel and Velchaninoff climbed into the carriage. "You must visit us again soon!" Their cheerful voices followed them as the carriage rolled away.

Chapter 13

Despite Velchaninoff's seemingly cheerful day, the irritation and sadness deep in his heart had never fully gone away, not even for a moment. Before singing the song, he had felt utterly restless, struggling with bottled-up anger and sorrow. Perhaps that was why his performance had been so heartfelt and passionate.

"To think I've sunk so low as to forget everything!" he thought to himself, then immediately scorned himself for even having such a thought. "But it's even more pathetic to dwell on what's already done," he continued. "It's better to let my anger out on someone instead."

"Idiot!" he muttered, casting a sideways glance at Pavel Pavlovitch, who sat beside him, quiet as a mouse. Pavel remained obstinately silent, as if gathering his strength and organizing his thoughts. Every so often, he impatiently took off his hat to wipe the sweat from his forehead.

Only once during the ride did Pavel Pavlovitch speak, and that was to the coachman. He asked if there was likely to be a thunderstorm.

"Oh, definitely," the man replied. "It's been such a heavy, humid day—just the kind for it."

By the time they reached the town, around half-past ten, the entire sky was covered in dark clouds.

"I'm coming to your place," Pavel Pavlovitch said to Velchaninoff as they neared his door.

"All right," Velchaninoff replied. "But I'm warning you, I'm not feeling well tonight."

"Don't worry—I won't stay long."

As they passed through the gateway, Pavel Pavlovitch ducked into the porter's room for a moment to speak to Mavra.

"What did you go in there for?" Velchaninoff asked sharply as they climbed the stairs to his apartment.

"Oh, nothing—nothing at all. Just to mention something about the coachman."

"Fine. But I'm telling you now, I won't let you drink!"

Pavel Pavlovitch said nothing.

Velchaninoff lit a candle while Pavel sank into a chair. Then Velchaninoff stepped forward, standing in front of him with a threatening demeanor.

"I told you earlier I'd have something to say tonight, just like you. Well, here it is," Velchaninoff said, his voice low but laced with anger. "As far as I'm concerned, everything between us is settled. There's nothing left to discuss. So, with that said, wouldn't it be best if you left and let me close the door behind you?"

"Let's call it even first, Alexey Ivanovitch," Pavel Pavlovitch replied, looking up at him with an oddly sweet expression.

"Even?" Velchaninoff repeated, stunned. "You're a strange man. What exactly are we supposed to be even about? Are you clinging to that 'last word' you promised?"

"Yes."

"Well, there's nothing left to settle between us. We've been even for a long time," Velchaninoff said firmly.

"Do you really mean that?" Pavel Pavlovitch cried out sharply, his voice high-pitched and strained. He clasped his hands tightly together, fingers interlocking, and held them up before his chest as though pleading.

Velchaninoff didn't respond right away. He got up and began pacing the room, his steps measured but tense. The name "Liza" echoed through his mind like the resonant toll of a heavy bell, striking deep into his core.

"What exactly do you think remains unresolved between us?" he asked finally, stopping abruptly to glare at Pavel. The latter hadn't moved or taken his eyes off Velchaninoff, his hands still pressed together in that peculiar, prayer-like gesture.

"Don't go back there again," Pavel murmured, his voice barely audible, as he stood up and seemed to shrink into himself, a picture of humble supplication.

"That's it? That's all you wanted to say?" Velchaninoff exclaimed, letting out an irritated laugh that bordered on a sneer. "Good grief, man, you've done nothing but shock me all day." He started with a tone of exasperation but then seemed to soften, his expression shifting to one of introspection and even a touch of vulnerability. "Listen to me," he said with deliberate emphasis. "I don't think I've ever felt as humiliated as I do today, after everything that's happened. First, that I allowed myself to be dragged along with you at all. And then, all that nonsense down there." His voice grew heavy with contempt. "What a day it's been—a day filled with nothing but petty, degrading foolishness. I stooped so low as to involve myself in it, and for what? For what?" He paused, rubbing his temple as though trying to chase away the bitter memory. "But it's done now. Done! And as for you, you blindsided me today when I was already unwell. So don't even try to make excuses. I'll tell you one thing for sure: I will not be going back there. I have no reason to."

"Really?" Pavel Pavlovitch's face lit up with a poorly concealed gleam of triumph. "You mean that?"

Velchaninoff cast him a look of utter disdain and resumed pacing the room, his movements brisker, more agitated now.

"You've decided to be happy, no matter what, haven't you?" he remarked disdainfully after a pause.

"Yes, I have," Pavel replied quietly but with an unnerving calm.

"It's absurd," Velchaninoff thought bitterly. "The man is both a fool and a scoundrel, but only because he's too stupid to be anything else. And yet, I hate him. Why? He's not even worth the effort of hating."

"I'm what you once called a 'permanent husband,'" Pavel suddenly declared, his tone oddly self-deprecating yet laced with irony. "Do you remember, Alexey Ivanovitch? You said that a long time ago, when you were visiting us in T——. I've always remembered that phrase of yours. And just the other day, when you brought it up again, it all came back to me."

At this point, Mavra entered with a bottle of champagne and two glasses.

"Forgive me, Alexey Ivanovitch," Pavel said apologetically, "but you know I can't seem to manage without it. Please, don't think me audacious—consider it nothing more than a harmless indulgence."

Velchaninoff grimaced. "Fine," he muttered, disgust evident in his tone. "But I'll remind you again—I'm not feeling well."

"One moment, just one," Pavel said hurriedly. "I'll drink one glass, and then I'll leave. My throat is parched."

He snatched the bottle, poured himself a glass, and drained it in a single gulp. Then he sat back down, looking at Velchaninoff with an unsettling expression that bordered on affection.

"What an unpleasant creature," Velchaninoff thought to himself with a shudder.

"She's young, you see," Pavel began again suddenly, his voice animated. "It's her friends that have influenced her, shaped her behavior. But she'll change. I'll be her servant if that's what it takes. She'll see a bit of society, experience a little of the world. It'll transform her completely."

Velchaninoff absently reached into his pocket, his fingers brushing against the case holding the bracelet. "I must remember to give this back to him," he thought grimly.

"You mentioned earlier that I've decided to be happy," Pavel continued earnestly, almost imploringly. "And yes, I have. I must marry again, Alexey Ivanovitch. If I don't, what will become of me?" He gestured toward the bottle on the table, his voice trembling slightly. "This is just a small part of what I've stooped to. Without a wife— without someone to believe in—I'll lose myself entirely. I need a new faith, a new purpose. If I can just believe in someone again, I'll rise. I'll be saved."

Velchaninoff couldn't help himself; he let out a short laugh, almost in disbelief. "Why are you telling me this?" he asked, his tone caught between mockery and genuine puzzlement.

Pavel hesitated, his face flushing slightly. "I—I wanted to see—" he stammered.

"To see what?"

"The effect, sir," Pavel admitted, now visibly flustered. "You see, I've only known her for a week, and when I met you yesterday, I thought... I thought it would be good to see her in a different light. To observe her in the company of another man. It's a foolish idea, I know. But I—well, I was curious. I wanted to test her nature."

Velchaninoff stared at him, stunned into silence. "You can't be serious," he muttered finally.

Pavel didn't flinch. "I see now that it was all just her youthful innocence," he continued, his tone softening. "And maybe a bit of influence from her friends. Alexey Ivanovitch, please forgive me for how I acted today. I swear, it won't happen again."

"Well, it certainly won't, because I won't be there," Velchaninoff replied with a wry laugh.

"That's partly why I'm saying it," Pavel admitted, lowering his gaze.

Velchaninoff shook his head in exasperation. "There's no limit to your absurdity," he said quietly, resuming his pacing.

Pavel Pavlovitch's chin began to tremble uncontrollably. His face contorted, and his lips quivered in a way that sent a cold chill through Velchaninoff. The sudden shift in Pavel's demeanor unsettled him deeply, leaving him unsure whether he was witnessing pain, anger, or something far worse. This tone, this unexpected vulnerability—or was it a calculated act?—had to be stopped immediately.

"Enough, Pavel Pavlovitch!" Velchaninoff said at last, his voice low but sharp. His face flushed with embarrassment and irritation, as though Pavel's display had somehow implicated him in its absurdity. "Why—why—" Velchaninoff's voice rose without warning, cracking into a shout, "why do you come to a man like me, sick, exhausted, already half out of his mind with fever and troubles, and drag me down into this swamp of lies, delusions, shameful theatrics, and ridiculous, twisted nonsense! That's the worst part of all—how absurd and meaningless it all is!"

His voice broke off, but he didn't stop. He began pacing the room in quick, frantic steps, as though the motion could free him from his rising anger. "You know it's nonsense! We both know it's nonsense!

You're lying to me, lying to yourself—whether you realize it or not! Both of us are wretched, pitiful creatures! But if you want proof—proof that you don't love me, that you despise me, hate me—I'll give it to you right now!"

Pavel Pavlovitch looked startled, but he didn't speak. He merely watched Velchaninoff with wide, trembling eyes, his hands now clasped together, wringing nervously in front of his chest.

"You didn't take me down to see your bride because you were curious how she would behave in the company of other men," Velchaninoff thundered, stopping abruptly in his tracks and glaring at Pavel. "What an absurd excuse! You saw me yesterday, and some vile impulse took hold of you. You wanted to show me the girl, to parade her in front of me and say, 'Look at her! She's mine! Try if you dare!' That's all it was—a challenge. Whether you realized it or not, that's what it was. And such a challenge could only come from hatred! You hate me, Pavel Pavlovitch!"

Velchaninoff's voice shook with fury as he resumed pacing, his footsteps loud and unsteady. His outburst seemed to have taken on a life of its own, and he felt as though he were spiraling into the same pit of irrationality he had just accused Pavel of dragging him into. Every word he said heightened his sense of shame, and yet he couldn't stop himself.

"I only wanted peace between us, Alexey Ivanovitch," Pavel Pavlovitch said finally, his voice low and wavering, his trembling chin and quivering lips giving him a pitiful appearance.

The sight of him, his meekness, his tone, only infuriated Velchaninoff further. "Peace? Peace?" he roared. "Don't you dare talk to me about peace! You've latched onto me like a parasite, harassing me until I'm so worn out that I can't think straight, just to make me say or do something in my madness! Do you think we are the same, you and I? We are not! We belong to different worlds, Pavel Pavlovitch. Between us lies a grave!" His voice was cold now, almost a hiss, and he stopped walking abruptly, glaring at Pavel with blazing eyes.

Pavel Pavlovitch's face turned ashen, his features twisting as though in unbearable pain. He took a step forward, his hands trembling violently. "And how do you know what that grave means to me?" he whispered, his voice tight with emotion. "How do you know what it holds for me?" He struck his chest with his fist, his movements frantic, almost comical in their intensity. "Yes, there is a grave between us—but it means more to me, Alexey Ivanovitch, far more than it does to you. You can't understand! More—more—more!" Each repetition was accompanied by a frenzied thud of his fist against his chest.

At that moment, the sharp, insistent ringing of the doorbell shattered the tense silence. Both men froze, their eyes snapping toward the door. The bell rang again, louder this time, as though whoever was outside had no intention of waiting.

"People don't ring like that for me," Velchaninoff muttered, his voice dripping with irritation.

"They don't ring like that for me, either!" Pavel Pavlovitch exclaimed anxiously. He had instantly shrunk back into his timid, cowering self, his earlier fervor extinguished as if it had never existed.

Velchaninoff scowled and strode to the door. Opening it, he found himself face-to-face with a young man, sharp and confident, his manner bordering on arrogance.

"Mr. Velchaninoff, I presume?" the young man said crisply.

"What is it?" Velchaninoff asked curtly, his irritation boiling over.

"I've been informed that Mr. Trusotsky is here," the man replied, glancing past Velchaninoff into the room. "I must see him immediately."

For a moment, Velchaninoff considered slamming the door in the man's face. But then he thought better of it, stepping aside with a tight-lipped grimace. "Come in. Mr. Trusotsky is here."

Chapter 14

A young man, no older than nineteen but perhaps even younger judging by his smooth, self-assured face, strode into the room with a sense of purpose. His dark eyes gleamed with confidence, almost defiance, and his thick black hair framed his striking features. Yet, there was a slight imperfection—his nose, a bit broad and upturned, prevented him from being truly handsome. Despite this, he carried himself with a flair that suggested he considered himself quite the presence.

He was well-dressed, though not extravagantly so, and his clothes fit him neatly, adding to his polished appearance. There was a slight theatricality to his manner, as if every gesture and word were part of a performance. Upon entering, he surveyed the room with an air of cool detachment, his posture upright and self-assured, as though the very space were his stage.

"I believe I have the opportunity of addressing Mr. Trusotsky?" he began, his voice deliberate, almost clipped. He placed particular emphasis on the word "opportunity," as if to underline that any interaction with Pavel Pavlovitch was, for him, more obligation than privilege. His tone carried a faint edge of mockery, subtle but unmistakable. Velchaninoff, observing from the side, quickly grasped the dynamic at play. He sensed the undercurrent of antagonism, and Pavel Pavlovitch seemed to pick up on it too, his expression tightening into one of wary alertness.

Pavel, however, refused to cower. "Not having the pleasure of your acquaintance," he replied evenly, though with a hint of ice in his tone, "I fail to see what business you might have with me."

The young man raised an eyebrow, clearly unimpressed. With calculated leisure, he reached into his pocket, drew out a pair of tortoiseshell glasses, and perched them on his nose. He directed his gaze toward a champagne bottle on the table, inspecting it as though it were an artifact of great interest. Only after a long, deliberate moment did he remove the glasses, pocket them again, and return his gaze to Pavel.

"Alexander Loboff," he said finally, as though presenting himself were a mere formality.

"What of it?" Pavel Pavlovitch asked, his voice clipped.

"That's my name. You haven't heard of me?" Loboff's tone implied that the answer was irrelevant, but he asked the question nonetheless.

"No," Pavel replied curtly.

"Well, I suppose there's no reason you should have. Still, I'm here on a matter of some importance regarding yourself." Loboff glanced around the room, his eyes lingering briefly on a chair. "I assume I may sit? I'm tired."

Before Pavel could respond, Velchaninoff stepped in, gesturing toward the chair. "Oh, please, by all means," he said, though the young man had already seated himself, crossing one leg over the other with casual confidence.

Pavel Pavlovitch remained standing, his hands clasped behind his back. His face betrayed no emotion, but there was a tension in his stance, a rigidity that suggested he was bracing himself.

"You might want to take a seat as well," Loboff remarked nonchalantly, nodding toward an empty chair. The suggestion was more an order than an offer, delivered with the faintest curl of his lips.

"Thank you," Pavel replied coolly, "but I prefer to stand."

"As you like, though I doubt you'll last long. Standing gets tiring," Loboff said with a shrug before turning to Velchaninoff. "You don't need to leave. In fact, I'd prefer if you stayed. Nadejda Fedosievna has spoken quite highly of you."

Velchaninoff arched an eyebrow. "Has she now? I don't see how she could have had the time."

"Oh, she found the time—immediately after you left." Loboff redirected his attention to Pavel, his tone shifting to one of brisk efficiency. "Now, Mr. Trusotsky, let me get straight to the point. Nadejda Fedosievna and I have long been in love. Our engagement has been an understanding between us for quite some time. Your sudden appearance has disrupted things. I am here to inform you, plainly, that you need to step aside. Immediately. Are you prepared to do so?"

Pavel Pavlovitch visibly stiffened, his face paling. For a moment, he was too stunned to respond, but then a spiteful smile twisted his lips. "Not in the slightest," he said, his voice calm but edged with venom.

Loboff didn't seem fazed. He leaned back in his chair, adjusting his posture as though settling in for a long conversation. "I see," he remarked, his tone light but laced with condescension. "Well, I suppose I expected as much. Still, I must insist. This isn't just about me, you see. It's about Nadejda Fedosievna, the woman you have so shamelessly imposed yourself upon. That alone warrants an explanation."

Pavel's eyes narrowed, his expression hardening. "I still don't see why I should continue listening to you. I don't even know who you are."

"You know perfectly well who I am," Loboff countered smoothly. "I introduced myself not five minutes ago. And you also know what I'm here to discuss. This is not a matter you can brush aside. Not to mention, your behavior toward Nadejda is appallingly presumptuous."

He delivered the statement with such effortless authority that it felt less like an accusation and more like an irrefutable fact. Pavel opened his mouth to reply, but Loboff cut him off, his tone growing sharper.

"Excuse me, young man," Pavel began, his voice tinged with irritation. But those two words—"young man"—were a misstep. They struck a nerve, and Loboff's demeanor shifted instantly. His air of casual indifference gave way to something colder, more calculating.

Loboff's expression hardened at the words "young man," as though Pavel's attempt at condescension had pierced his composure. He leaned forward slightly, resting his elbows on his knees, and fixed Pavel with a steely glare. The confidence that had previously seemed playful now felt sharp, like a blade being unsheathed.

"Excuse me?" Loboff repeated, his voice low but taut. "Did you just call me 'young man'? Is that how you intend to address me during this conversation? Because if so, I'm afraid this discussion will end very quickly, and not in a way that benefits you."

Pavel Pavlovitch flinched but quickly recovered, his lips curving into a thin, spiteful smile. "Forgive me if my choice of words offended you. However, I fail to see why I should entertain this conversation any longer."

"Oh, you'll entertain it," Loboff retorted, his tone now icy. "Because this isn't just about me—it's about Nadejda Fedosievna. Do you think your presence in her life is welcome? Do you imagine she feels anything but revulsion when you're near her? You've overstepped your bounds, Mr. Trusotsky, and it's time you recognized that."

Pavel's pale face flushed slightly, but his voice remained steady. "You speak as though you have some authority in this matter. Let me remind you that Nadejda's family, not you, will ultimately decide her future."

Loboff's laughter was sharp and humorless. "The family? You think the Zachlebnikoffs see you as anything more than a temporary convenience? A suitor of financial advantage, at best? Let me assure you, they won't mourn your absence when you step aside."

Pavel's hand clenched the arm of his chair, his knuckles whitening. "You presume too much," he said tightly.

"And you presume too little," Loboff shot back. "You don't see what's plainly in front of you. Nadejda Fedosievna has no interest in you. She tolerates you out of duty, perhaps, but that's the extent of it. Meanwhile, I—" He paused, leaning back again, as though savoring the words to come. "I am the one she truly cares for. I am the one she loves. And that is why I am here—to ensure you understand your position clearly."

Velchaninoff, who had been observing the exchange with growing interest, could not suppress a smirk. The young man's audacity was almost entertaining, though Velchaninoff couldn't decide whether it was admirable or foolish. Still, he couldn't help but note the way Loboff's arguments seemed to cut straight to Pavel's insecurities.

Pavel Pavlovitch, for his part, looked increasingly cornered. His usual self-assurance seemed to falter under the weight of Loboff's accusations. He opened his mouth, closed it again, and finally managed to say, "You speak boldly for someone so young."

"I speak boldly because I have the truth on my side," Loboff replied without missing a beat. "And because I am not afraid to confront a man who is clearly unfit to be in Nadejda's life."

Velchaninoff's smirk deepened. He could see the storm brewing within Pavel, the way his composure teetered on the brink of collapse. For a moment, he wondered if Pavel would lash out physically, but instead, Pavel straightened in his chair, his face a mask of icy resolve.

"You may think you've won, young man," Pavel said quietly, his voice trembling with suppressed anger. "But let me assure you, this matter is far from settled. Nadejda's family values stability and tradition, not the impulsive whims of a boy barely out of school."

Loboff's smile returned, wider and sharper than before. "And yet here I am, sitting across from you, making my case while you squirm. If this is the best resistance you can offer, Mr. Trusotsky, I'd say your position is already lost."

Velchaninoff chuckled softly, drawing both men's attention. "Gentlemen," he said, spreading his hands in mock mediation. "While this is all very entertaining, I must say, you both seem to be forgetting the most important voice in this matter—Nadejda herself. Perhaps we should let her decide who she wishes to tolerate, if either of you."

The suggestion hung in the air for a moment, charged with tension. Pavel Pavlovitch glanced away, his expression dark and unreadable. Loboff, however, seemed emboldened, as though Velchaninoff's comment had validated his position.

"An excellent point," Loboff said, his tone triumphant. "And I have no doubt that, given the choice, she will make the right one."

Pavel rose abruptly, his chair scraping loudly against the floor. "This conversation is over," he said stiffly, his voice low but firm. "Good evening, gentlemen."

Without another word, he turned and strode toward the door, his movements rigid with barely contained fury. Loboff watched him go, a satisfied smirk playing on his lips, before turning back to Velchaninoff.

"Well," he said, leaning back in his chair with an air of victory. "That went about as expected."

Velchaninoff said nothing, but the faint amusement in his eyes spoke volumes. As the room fell silent, he couldn't help but marvel at the strange theater of human pride and folly that had just unfolded before him.

"At any other time," the young man began, his tone laced with smug self-assurance, "I would not have tolerated you calling me 'young man.' I would have corrected you on the spot. However, in this particular instance, my youth is actually my greatest advantage over you. In fact, I dare say that, even earlier today, you would have given anything—absolutely anything—to be just a few years younger, especially at the moment when you presented that bracelet."

"Cheeky brat," muttered Velchaninoff under his breath, unable to mask his annoyance.

Pavel Pavlovitch, striving to maintain his dignity, began to speak in a measured tone. "I must say, young sir, that the reasons you have presented are both questionable and entirely improper. They fail to justify the continuation of this conversation. I must therefore conclude that your 'business,' as you call it, is nothing more than immature nonsense. Tomorrow, I shall have the honor of discussing this matter with Mr. Zachlebnikoff himself, my esteemed friend. In the meantime, I would suggest that you kindly take your leave."

"That's exactly the kind of man he is!" Loboff shot back, his voice rising in anger. He turned to Velchaninoff as if seeking an ally. "Do you see? He's not content with being humiliated and having the girl openly show her disdain for him. No, he plans to go crawling back tomorrow to tattle to Mr. Zachlebnikoff! Isn't it obvious that his intention is to forcefully take control of Nadejda, as though she were some commodity to be bargained for? He clings to the outdated notion that her family's authority over her gives him the right to impose himself. And as if that weren't enough, he had the audacity to give her that tasteless, wretched bracelet today. It's been returned to him—what more does he want?"

"Excuse me," Pavel Pavlovitch interjected, his face growing pale as he struggled to contain his rising anxiety. "No bracelet has been returned to me, nor could it have been."

"What do you mean? Hasn't Mr. Velchaninoff given it to you yet?" Loboff asked sharply, his eyes narrowing in suspicion.

Velchaninoff sighed, his frustration mounting. "Nadejda Fedosievna did indeed give me the bracelet case to return to you, Pavel Pavlovitch," he admitted reluctantly. "I didn't want to take it, but she insisted. Here it is. I'm very sorry." He retrieved the small case from his pocket and placed it on the table before Pavel, whose expression shifted from shock to barely concealed fury.

"And why, may I ask, did you not hand it over sooner?" Loboff inquired, his tone tinged with accusation.

"I had no time, as you may have guessed," Velchaninoff replied curtly, frowning.

"Hmm, a strange delay," Loboff remarked, his suspicion evident.

"What exactly do you find strange about it?" Velchaninoff retorted, his patience wearing thin.

"Well, it's just unusual, that's all," the young man said with a smirk. "However, I'm willing to believe there was some innocent misunderstanding."

Velchaninoff felt a surge of irritation. The audacity of this young man was almost too much to bear. He would have gladly thrown him out of the house by the ear, but instead, to his own surprise, he burst into laughter. The sound seemed to disarm Loboff, who joined in with a laugh of his own.

But Pavel Pavlovitch was far from amused. His face darkened as he glared at the two of them, his lips twitching with barely suppressed rage. If Velchaninoff had noticed the ferocity in Pavel's eyes at that moment, he might have realized how close the man was to losing all self-control. Oblivious, Velchaninoff decided it was time to intervene on Pavel's behalf.

"Mr. Loboff," Velchaninoff began in a conciliatory tone, "let's set aside these other matters for a moment. Allow me to point out that Mr. Trusotsky brings with him, in his pursuit of Miss Zachlebnikoff, a name and a standing that are well known and respected by her family. He also offers a stable position and considerable wealth. Given these factors, you must understand why he may find it difficult to view someone of your age as a serious rival."

"What do you mean by 'my age'?" Loboff interrupted, his voice rising defensively. "I turned nineteen last month. By law, I've been eligible for marriage for quite some time. That alone refutes your argument."

"Even so," Velchaninoff countered calmly, "what father would allow his daughter to marry someone so young, regardless of the law? While you may have potential, a man of nineteen is still finding his way in life. Taking on the responsibility of a wife—who, I might add, is as young and inexperienced as yourself—is hardly prudent or even honorable. Surely you can see how this could be viewed as impulsive, if not irresponsible."

Loboff snorted dismissively. "Impulsive? Irresponsible? What nonsense! You assume too much. Let me tell you something—Nadejda and I have pledged ourselves to each other. Moreover, I've given her my solemn word that she may break off our engagement at any time if she so chooses. I've even ensured that this promise was witnessed by others."

Velchaninoff couldn't suppress a mocking laugh. "I'd wager that was Predposiloff's idea, wasn't it?"

"It was," Loboff admitted without hesitation. "But what of it? I don't expect you to understand. Frankly, I find it disappointing that someone described to me as a man of originality should resort to such outdated reasoning. How old are you, anyway? Fifty?"

"Stick to the subject at hand," Velchaninoff snapped, his tone sharp.

"Of course. I meant no offense," Loboff replied with exaggerated politeness. "But to return to the matter, I may not be wealthy or a great benefactor to humanity—yet—but I can provide for myself and my wife. You see, I was raised in their household, practically as one of their own."

"How so?" Velchaninoff asked, his curiosity piqued despite himself.

Loboff leaned back, a triumphant glint in his eye, ready to launch into his next argument. Pavel Pavlovitch, meanwhile, sat stiffly in his chair, his knuckles white as he gripped the armrests, his rage simmering just beneath the surface.

"Oh, it's because I'm a distant relative of Mr. Zachlebnikoff's wife. When my parents died, he took me in and sent me to school. The old man really has a kind heart, if you knew him."

"I do know it!" replied Velchaninoff.

"Yes, he's a bit of an old fogey, but a kind-hearted one. Still, I left his house about four months ago and started supporting myself. At first, I worked at a railway office for ten roubles a month. Now I'm earning twenty-five as a clerk in a notary's office. Two weeks ago, I officially proposed to Nadia. At first, he laughed like crazy, but then he got furious, and Nadia was locked up. She endured it bravely. He was already mad at me for quitting a job he had secured for me in his department. You see, he's a good, kind man at home, but at work—oh, my word!—he turns into a complete tyrant! I told him outright that I didn't care for his ways. That caused a huge argument, thanks to the second-in-command at the office. He claimed I insulted him, but all I said was that he was an ignorant fool. So I quit the department and decided to try my luck in notary work instead. Listen to that thunder! It's going to storm any minute now. Good thing I made it here before the rain started! I came on foot, you know—nearly ran the whole way!"

"How did you manage to talk to Miss Nadia then? Especially since you're not allowed to meet her."

"Oh, there's always a way! You can climb over the railing. Then there's that red-haired girl—she helps, and so does Maria Nikitishna. But, oh, she's a snake, that one! What's wrong? Are you afraid of the storm?"

"No, I'm just ill—seriously ill!" Velchaninoff stood up, clutching his chest as a sharp pain overtook him. He tried pacing the room to ease the discomfort.

"Oh, really! Then I'm bothering you. I'll leave right away," said the young man, springing to his feet.

"No, you're not disturbing me," Velchaninoff replied stiffly, trying to maintain a formal tone.

"Of course I am! You're sick, probably with a stomachache. Well then, Pavel Pavlovitch, let's wrap this up. I'll make my point clear and simple, so there's no misunderstanding: Are you prepared to renounce your claim to Nadejda Fedosievna's hand in marriage, in front of her parents and me, with full formality?"

"No, sir, I am not in the slightest bit prepared," Pavel Pavlovitch retorted coldly. "And let me say again, all this is childish and absurd. You should leave now."

"Careful," warned the young man, raising a finger. "You'd better give it up while you can, or you'll waste a fortune and a lot of effort. When you come back in nine months, Nadia herself will turn you out of the house. And if you don't leave then, things will get much worse for you. Don't take this as a threat, but as advice. Right now, you're like a dog in the manger. Think about it and make a wise choice for once in your life."

"Spare me your lectures!" Pavel Pavlovitch shouted, his fury rising. "As for your pathetic threats, I'll take measures tomorrow—serious measures!"

"Pathetic threats?" the youth sneered. "It's pathetic of you to even see them as threats. Fine, I'll wait until tomorrow. But mark my words—" A loud clap of thunder interrupted him. "There it is again! Well, au revoir! It's been a pleasure meeting you, sir," he said with a nod toward Velchaninoff.

With that, he turned and left in a hurry, eager to reach home before the rain began.

Chapter 15

"You see, you see!" Pavel cried to Velchaninoff the moment the young man turned his back.

"Yes, it's clear you're not going to have much luck there," replied Velchaninoff. His tone was abrupt, not out of malice but because of the sharp, unbearable pain in his chest.

Pavel Pavlovitch flinched, as though someone had thrown boiling water on him. "Well, sir, and you—you didn't seem too eager to return the bracelet, did you?"

"I didn't have time."

"Oh! You felt sorry for me—you pitied me, like a true friend pities a friend!"

"Fine, then—I pitied you," Velchaninoff snapped, growing angrier by the second. He quickly explained how he came to have the bracelet, recounting how Nadia had practically forced it into his hands.

"You have to understand," he added, "that otherwise I wouldn't have taken on the task. There's already enough unpleasantness as it is."

"You enjoyed it; you took it on gladly," Pavel Pavlovitch giggled, though there was a bitterness in his voice.

"That's a ridiculous thing to say. But I suppose you can't help yourself. You must have noticed from that boy's behavior that I have no role in this matter. Others are at the center of it all, not me!"

"Still, the job seemed to appeal to you," Pavel said as he settled into his seat and poured himself a glass of wine.

"You think I'll let that boy have the last word? Ridiculous! Tomorrow, I'll send him packing like the useless brat he is. I'll smoke him out of his little nursery, just watch!" He downed the wine in one gulp and poured another, seeming to grow bolder with every sip.

"Ha-ha! Little Sasha and Nadya! Sweet little children, aren't they? Ha-ha-ha!" His laughter carried a sharp edge, brimming with rage.

Just then, a deafening clap of thunder shattered the stillness, followed by bright flashes of lightning and heavy sheets of rain. Pavel Pavlovitch got up to close the window.

"Remember when he asked if you were afraid of the thunder? Ha-ha-ha! Velchaninoff, afraid of thunder! And that part about you being 'fifty years old'—that wasn't bad, eh? Ha-ha-ha!" Pavel's voice was laced with malice.

"You seem quite comfortable here," Velchaninoff muttered, struggling to speak through his pain. "Do whatever you want. I need to lie down."

"Oh, come on, you wouldn't throw a dog out on a night like this!" Pavel said, seizing on the chance to play the victim.

"Fine, stay, drink your wine, do whatever pleases you," Velchaninoff murmured as he collapsed onto his divan, groaning in agony.

"Should I spend the night? Aren't you afraid?"

"Afraid of what?" Velchaninoff asked, lifting his head slightly.

"Oh, nothing. It's just that last time, you seemed a bit nervous, that's all."

"You're an idiot!" Velchaninoff barked, turning his face to the wall.

"Very well, sir; as you wish," Pavel replied quietly.

Velchaninoff fell asleep almost immediately after lying down. The strain of the day, combined with his poor health, had left him utterly drained, as weak as a child. But the physical pain soon overpowered his exhaustion and forced him awake. Within an hour, he was up again, pacing in agony. Pavel Pavlovitch was sound asleep on the other sofa, fully dressed with his boots on. His hat lay on the floor, and his eyeglasses dangled from their cord almost to the ground. Velchaninoff didn't wake him. The room reeked of tobacco, and the empty wine bottle sat on the table. He cast a furious glance at the sleeping man, disgusted.

Unable to bear lying down any longer, Velchaninoff dragged himself up, groaning as he walked around the room. The pain in his chest was unbearable, and he couldn't ignore it. These attacks were rare, occurring only once every year or two, but when they struck, the agony was overwhelming, lasting for hours. Tonight's attack was one of the worst he had ever experienced. It was too late to call a doctor, and morning was still far off. He stumbled back and forth, his groans growing louder and more frequent as the pain deepened.

His noise finally woke Pavel Pavlovitch, who sat up on the sofa, blinking in confusion. For a moment, he stared at Velchaninoff in terror, as though unsure of what he was seeing. When he regained his senses, he asked, his voice shaking, what was wrong.

Velchaninoff muttered something incomprehensible.

"It's your kidneys—I'm sure of it!" Pavel exclaimed, suddenly wide awake. "I remember Peter Kuzmich had the same thing. Kidney trouble—it can be deadly! Let me fetch Mavra."

"No, no, I don't need anything," Velchaninoff replied, waving him off irritably.

But for reasons unknown, Pavel Pavlovitch was overcome with concern, acting as if Velchaninoff's life depended on his quick thinking.

He insisted on treating the pain immediately. He decided hot compresses and scalding tea would help. Ignoring Velchaninoff's protests, Pavel rushed to wake Mavra, lit the kitchen stove, boiled water, and prepared everything himself. He guided Velchaninoff back to bed, covering him up securely. In less than twenty minutes, he had the first hot compress ready, along with a steaming cup of tea.

"Hot plates will do the trick!" Pavel declared, wrapping a heated plate in a napkin and pressing it against Velchaninoff's chest. "I don't have anything else handy, but this will work just as well. Now drink this tea—don't worry if it burns your tongue. Your life's more important. You can't take risks with this sort of thing!" He sent Mavra scurrying about in a panic to keep up with his demands. Every couple of minutes, he replaced the plates with fresh ones. After the third compress and two cups of scorching tea, Velchaninoff finally felt some relief.

"Excellent! Thank God! If we've managed to ease the pain, that's a very good sign!" Pavel exclaimed, overjoyed. He rushed to fetch more plates and tea, muttering, "We just need to keep fighting the pain."

Within half an hour, the worst of the pain had subsided. Velchaninoff, utterly exhausted, could no longer endure any more treatment. Despite Pavel's pleas to apply "just one more plate," he weakly waved him off.

"Sleep—just let me sleep," he murmured faintly, his eyes closing.

"All right, all right. Sleep," Pavel agreed softly. "Go ahead and rest."

"Are you staying here tonight? What time is it?" Velchaninoff asked.

"Almost two," Pavel replied. "Yes, I'll stay here."

"Good," Velchaninoff mumbled, already drifting off.

Moments later, he stirred again and muttered something faintly as Pavel approached, bending down to listen.

"You... you're better than me," Velchaninoff said, his voice barely audible. "I understand... everything. Thank you."

"Go to sleep," Pavel whispered, retreating to the other sofa.

As Velchaninoff began to doze, he heard Pavel quietly making his own bed. The man undressed with care, lay down softly, and turned out the light.

Velchaninoff drifted off into sleep almost as soon as the light was extinguished. Later, he would remember falling asleep easily, but during the night, he dreamed he couldn't sleep at all, despite his exhaustion. In the dream, he imagined himself delirious, surrounded by visions he couldn't escape. Although he knew these were only illusions and not reality, they seemed to take control of him.

In this vision, he saw his front door wide open, and people began to flood into the room, filling it. In the center of the room, seated at the table, was a man leaning on his elbow. This figure reminded Velchaninoff of a dream he had a month before. Just like in that earlier dream, the man was silent, wearing a round hat with a black crape band.

"Wait," Velchaninoff thought. "Was it Pavel Pavlovitch in the dream before, too?" But when he looked closer at the man's face, he realized it was someone else entirely.

"Then why does he have a crape band?" Velchaninoff wondered, more confused than ever.

The room grew louder as the crowd chattered angrily. Their voices blended into a deafening roar, and they seemed furious with him. Fists waved in the air, and shouts filled the room. They were yelling something, but he couldn't make out their words.

"This is just a dream," Velchaninoff thought to himself, though uneasily. "I know it's a dream because I'd never be lying still. I'd be pacing around because of the pain."

But the noise, the shouting, and the intensity of the scene felt so vivid that he began to doubt himself.

"Could this really be delirium?" he thought, panic rising. "What do all these people want from me? My God, what do they want?"

If it wasn't a dream, wouldn't all this noise have woken Pavel Pavlovitch? Velchaninoff glanced over at the other sofa, where Pavel lay sleeping, oblivious to the chaos.

Then, just like in his earlier dream, there was a shift. A new group of people barged in, forcing their way through the already crowded room. They were carrying something large and heavy. The noise of their feet on the stairs revealed just how much effort it took to bring it up.

"They're bringing it!" shouted the people in the room, their eyes glowing with excitement as they turned to Velchaninoff. Their hands pointed at him and then towards the stairs.

He felt his heart pounding wildly, his breath quickening. The scene felt so real that he became certain it wasn't a dream. Velchaninoff thought he stood up and stretched on tiptoes to see over the crowd, desperate to catch a glimpse of what they were bringing in.

Just as before, three sharp, loud rings at the bell shattered the noise. The sound was so vivid, so clear, that Velchaninoff was sure it couldn't be a dream. He cried out and woke with a start, but unlike the last time, he didn't rush to the door.

Instead, he reacted instinctively, moving without thought. He sprang out of bed, arms stretched forward as if to shield himself, and turned straight toward the divan where Pavel Pavlovitch lay.

His hands met resistance—another pair of hands reaching out toward him. Someone was standing over him.

Although the curtains were drawn, a faint light seeped in from the next room, making it just light enough to see shapes.

Suddenly, Velchaninoff felt something sharp cut into the palm of his left hand. The sting spread through his fingers, and he realized he had grabbed onto a knife or a razor. With lightning speed, he clenched it tightly, his reflexes taking over.

In the next moment, something metallic clattered to the floor.

Though Velchaninoff was far stronger than Pavel Pavlovitch, the struggle between them dragged on for what felt like an eternity—three long minutes at least. Velchaninoff finally forced Pavel to the ground, pinning his arms behind his head.

Panting, Velchaninoff hesitated. He needed something to tie Pavel's hands. Clutching Pavel's wrist tightly with his injured left hand, he reached around with his right, fumbling for something—anything. His fingers eventually found the window blind cord, and he yanked it down with a sharp pull.

He couldn't believe the unnatural strength he must have used during the struggle. Later, this realization amazed him.

Neither of them spoke a word as they fought. The only sounds in the room were their heavy breathing and the grunts and gasps they made during the struggle.

Finally, after securing Pavel Pavlovitch's hands, Velchaninoff left him on the floor, stood up, and drew the curtains aside. He raised the blind to let in the first light of dawn.

The street outside was silent and empty, lit faintly by the early morning. Velchaninoff opened the window and stood there for a moment, breathing in the cool, fresh air. It was just past four o'clock. After a few moments, he closed the window, fetched a towel, and wrapped it tightly around his bleeding hand to stop the flow of blood.

As he moved, his eyes caught sight of the open razor lying on the carpet near his feet. He picked it up, wiped it clean, and placed it back into its case, which he now noticed sitting on the small cupboard near the divan Pavel Pavlovitch had been using. He locked the cupboard securely this time.

Once he had done all this, Velchaninoff approached Pavel Pavlovitch and studied him closely. By now, Pavel had managed to get himself up from the floor and was sitting in a chair. He was undressed except for his shirt, which was stained with blood on both the front and the back—but the blood wasn't his; it was Velchaninoff's.

There was no mistaking that it was Pavel Pavlovitch sitting there, but anyone who had known him before would have doubted it was the same man. His posture was stiff and awkward because his hands were tightly tied behind his back. His face was pale and distorted, and he shivered every few moments. His expression was a mixture of dazed confusion and intense focus as he stared at Velchaninoff.

Suddenly, Pavel smiled faintly and nodded toward the water carafe on the table. "A little drop," he muttered. Velchaninoff poured some water into a glass and held it to him so he could drink.

Pavel gulped down two mouthfuls quickly. Then he lifted his head and stared intently at Velchaninoff, who was still standing over him. He didn't say a word but finished drinking the water and then let out a deep sigh.

Velchaninoff gathered his pillows and a few items of clothing and moved into the adjoining room. He locked the door behind him, leaving Pavel Pavlovitch alone in the other room.

The sharp pain in his chest had finally subsided, but he felt drained of energy after the physical and emotional strain he had endured. He couldn't fathom where his strength had come from during the struggle. He tried to think about it, but his thoughts were scattered, his mind too overwhelmed by the shock of what had just happened.

Every so often, his eyes would close, and he would drift off for a few minutes, only to wake with a start, remembering everything. He would glance at the bloodied towel wrapped around his hand, as if to reassure himself that what had happened wasn't just some terrible nightmare. Then he would sink back into restless thoughts.

One thing was clear: Pavel Pavlovitch had intended to kill him. The attempt might not have been premeditated; it seemed more likely that Pavel hadn't even known he would try until moments before the attack. Perhaps he had noticed the razor case the night before without thinking much of it, only to remember it later. Normally, Velchaninoff kept the razors locked away, but yesterday, he had taken one out to shave before his trip and had forgotten to lock it back up.

"If he had truly planned this in advance," Velchaninoff reasoned, "he would have brought his own weapon, like a knife or a pistol. He couldn't have relied on my razors, which he only saw yesterday."

As the clock struck six, Velchaninoff stood up, dressed quickly, and went to Pavel Pavlovitch's room. He hesitated as he unlocked the door, wondering why he had locked it in the first place and why he hadn't simply let Pavel leave the night before.

To his surprise, Pavel Pavlovitch was already dressed. He had somehow freed his hands. He sat in an armchair but stood up as soon as Velchaninoff entered. His hat was in his hand, and his anxious expression seemed to plead silently: "Don't say anything. There's no point. Just let me go."

"Go," Velchaninoff said curtly. Then he added, "Take your jewel case."

Pavel Pavlovitch turned, grabbed the bracelet case from the table, stuffed it into his pocket, and walked out.

Velchaninoff followed him to the hall, standing there to make sure he left. Their eyes met for a long moment before Pavel reached the door. They stared at each other, as though each was trying to decide whether to say something. Finally, Velchaninoff raised a hand in a faint, dismissive gesture.

"Go," he repeated, this time in a quieter voice. Then he closed the door behind Pavel and locked it.

Chapter 16

Velchaninoff felt a deep sense of relief, an overwhelming happiness as if a heavy burden had been lifted from his shoulders. Something that had consumed him for five long weeks was finally over, done with, and resolved.

He raised his hand and looked at the bloodstained rag wrapped tightly around it.

"Oh, yes," he thought to himself, "it really is over now."

For the first time in many days, his mind didn't wander to Liza. It was as if the blood from his wounded fingers had somehow washed away that particular sorrow, making him feel like he had finally settled his score with the past.

He understood how close he had come to losing his life.

"People like him," he thought, "don't plan to kill you until the very last moment. But once they feel the knife in their hands and the warmth of blood, they can't stop. They don't just cut your throat; they'd hack your head off completely."

He couldn't stay at home. Restless and anxious, he needed to go out, to do something, to let the world happen around him. He walked aimlessly, hoping for anything to distract him. He thought of visiting a doctor to have his hand properly bandaged and maybe talk to him—it seemed like as good an idea as any.

At the doctor's office, when asked how he had hurt his hand, Velchaninoff couldn't help but laugh. The urge to spill everything surged up within him, but he managed to hold back. Several times that day, he felt the same urge to share his story, even with complete strangers. Once, in a restaurant, he almost confided in a man he had never met before, someone he had struck up a conversation with on a whim. Normally, he hated talking to strangers in public places, but today was different.

Later, he visited a shop and ordered new clothes, not because he intended to visit the Pogoryeltseffs but simply because the idea of leaving town didn't appeal to him. He felt an inexplicable need to stay in the city, to see what might unfold.

Dinner was surprisingly pleasant. He enjoyed his meal and chatted easily with both his neighbor and the waiter. As evening fell, he returned home feeling slightly light-headed, almost as if he were on the verge of delirium. The sight of his rooms startled him for a moment, stirring strange feelings. He wandered through them slowly, stopping in the kitchen—a place he rarely visited.

"This is where they heated the plates last night," he thought absently.

He locked the doors carefully and lit the candles earlier than usual. Passing by the dvornik's lodging on his way in, he had casually asked Mavra whether Pavel Pavlovitch had come by. The question now seemed absurd—of course, Pavel wouldn't be anywhere near the place.

Once inside, he opened the cupboard where he kept his razors and took out the one that had been used. There was still dried blood on its handle. He cleaned it, put it back in its case, and locked the cupboard tightly this time.

Feeling exhausted, he knew he needed sleep. Tomorrow seemed important, though he couldn't explain why. Something about it felt significant, fateful even. Yet, despite his fatigue, he couldn't quiet his thoughts. All the events of the day replayed endlessly in his mind, making sleep impossible.

The question haunted him: had Pavel Pavlovitch ever consciously thought of murder before the attack? Velchaninoff came to a strange conclusion: Pavel had wanted to kill him but didn't realize it himself until the moment it happened.

"It's a ridiculous idea, but it must be true," he thought.

Pavel Pavlovitch hadn't come to St. Petersburg to find a new job or because of Bagantoff, despite his fury when the man died. Pavel had despised Bagantoff. No, Pavel had come to St. Petersburg because of him, Velchaninoff. He had even brought Liza along, and it was all because of him.

Velchaninoff couldn't stop the thoughts racing through his mind. "Did I actually expect him to try and kill me?" he wondered. He decided that, in some way, he had expected something terrible to happen ever since he saw Pavel Pavlovitch in the carriage following Bagantoff's funeral procession. "Of course, I didn't expect him to cut my throat specifically—but I knew something was bound to happen!"

His thoughts grew more intense. "And surely, surely, what he said yesterday wasn't entirely sincere," Velchaninoff thought as he raised his head from the pillow, stirred by this possibility. "Could he really have meant everything he said—professing his love for me, beating his chest, his lip trembling as he spoke?"

"Yes," he concluded after a moment. "It was entirely sincere. This strange man from T—— was absolutely capable of loving me, his wife's lover, with a bizarre kind of affection. And this was the same wife, mind you, whom he had lived with for twenty years without suspecting a thing."

Velchaninoff shook his head in disbelief. "He admired me for nine years, remembered my sayings, and thought so highly of me, while I, meanwhile, knew absolutely nothing of his feelings. No, he wasn't lying yesterday. But did he truly love me when he declared his love and said we had to settle accounts? Yes, he did. He loved me, but it was a spiteful kind of love—and spiteful love can sometimes be the strongest."

He began pacing the room as his thoughts raced on. "I must have left an enormous impression on him back in T——. People like him, with their overblown, romantic ideals, are often struck by someone they perceive as larger-than-life. He probably saw me as a thousand times greater than I actually was. Maybe it was my so-called 'philosophical detachment' that impressed him—or even something as trivial as how well I wore my gloves! These odd types often idolize people for the smallest reasons."

Velchaninoff smirked bitterly at the thought. "And once they start admiring you, they do all the work themselves—adding layer upon layer to the pedestal they build for you. They'll even fight for you, as though you're the epitome of every virtue. No wonder he felt so betrayed when he realized I wasn't the paragon he thought I was."

"And then," he mused, "he came here to 'embrace me and weep together,' as he put it. In reality, he came here to kill me but didn't realize it. He even brought Liza along, using her as part of his strange attempt to reconcile with me—or to punish me, maybe both."

Velchaninoff stopped pacing and rubbed his temples. "If I'd played along yesterday, weeping and embracing him, would he really have forgiven me? Maybe he would have, completely and wholeheartedly. But when things didn't go the way he'd hoped, everything fell apart. That desperate desire to forgive turned into drunkenness and rage. Yes, Pavel Pavlovitch, the saddest thing about you is that you're a man with noble feelings trapped inside a deformed and pitiful soul."

He shook his head again, thinking of Pavel's bizarre decision to take him to see Nadia. "What madness! His bride, of all people! Only someone as delusional as Pavel could dream up a new life for himself based on a union with a girl like Nadia. And yet, for some twisted reason, my approval was essential to him. Maybe he really believed that, in the presence of her innocence and charm, we'd reconcile and forgive each other in some idyllic moment."

Velchaninoff's mind circled back to earlier incidents. "Was he thinking of murder the night I caught him standing between our beds? No, I don't think so. But maybe the idea entered his mind then, creeping in like a shadow. And if I hadn't left those razors out, nothing would have happened. He even avoided me for weeks—probably because he felt sorry for me. That night with the hot plates, he was trying to distract himself, trying to suppress whatever dark impulse he was feeling."

His thoughts ran on and on, jumping from one conclusion to the next, until exhaustion finally overtook him and he fell asleep. But the morning brought no relief. He woke up with his body and mind still drained, and a strange new fear weighing on him.

This fear wasn't of Pavel Pavlovitch coming back to harm him. No, it was the overwhelming and inexplicable feeling that he had to go to Pavel Pavlovitch's lodging that very day. He couldn't explain it, but the urge was undeniable, as if some invisible force was pulling him there. The idea repelled him, yet he couldn't shake it.

He tried to rationalize this compulsion. Perhaps Pavel had gone home and done something drastic, like hanging himself. The thought of Pavel ending his life, as Liza had once described with such horror, took hold of Velchaninoff's mind.

"Why would he hang himself?" Velchaninoff asked himself over and over. "What would drive him to such an act?" Yet the thought persisted, and he couldn't help imagining that, if he were in Pavel's shoes, he might feel the same.

Finally, he decided to go, not to embrace Pavel or to reconcile with him, but simply to check on him. However, as he walked toward Pavel's lodging, his resolve wavered. By the time he reached the street, he stopped in his tracks, his face flushing with embarrassment.

"Am I really going there to weep over him?" he asked himself. "Am I about to add this ridiculous act to all the humiliations of the past days?"

But before he could answer his own question, fate intervened. As he entered the gateway, Alexander Loboff appeared out of nowhere, dashing toward him in a state of visible excitement.

Velchaninoff was startled when Alexander Loboff suddenly appeared and blurted, "I was just on my way to see you. Our friend Pavel Pavlovitch—what a character he is!"

"Has he hanged himself?" Velchaninoff interrupted, his voice shaking.

"Hanged himself? Who? What are you talking about?" Loboff asked, his eyes wide with confusion.

"Oh, never mind. Go on," Velchaninoff replied quickly, trying to cover up his outburst.

"Tfu! What strange thoughts you have! No, he hasn't hanged himself—not at all. On the contrary, he's left town. I just saw him off! My goodness, that man can drink! We had three bottles of wine. Predposiloff was there too. But, oh, how he drinks! He was singing in the train carriage as it departed! He even sent his regards to you— waved and kissed his hand. What a scoundrel he is, eh?"

Loboff's flushed face and slurred speech made it clear he had partaken generously in the wine. Velchaninoff burst out laughing.

"So, you ended up crying on each other's shoulders, did you? Ha! You romantic, theatrical fools!"

"Don't scold us. You know, he went back to see Nadia and me yesterday and again today. But he's backed off now. He was groveling about me and Nadia, trying to stir up trouble. They've locked her up, but we didn't give in. And wow, how that man can drink! He kept bringing you up, though. But honestly, he's not the kind of person you'd associate with. You seem like someone who's been part of high society—although now, it looks like you've stepped back. Is it because of money troubles or something? I couldn't really understand Pavel Pavlovitch's version of your story."

"Oh, so it was he who gave you those fascinating details about me?" Velchaninoff asked dryly.

"Yes, but don't take it the wrong way. I think it's better to be an ordinary citizen than a 'big shot.' The problem in Russia these days is that nobody knows who to respect. Don't you agree that it's a serious issue?"

"Quite so, quite so. Well, continue. What else about Pavel Pavlovitch?"

"Well, in the railway carriage, he started singing, then crying. Honestly, it was disgusting. I can't stand idiots like him. Then he began throwing money to beggars, saying it was 'for the repose of Liza's soul.' Is she his wife?"

"His daughter."

"What happened to your hand?"

"I cut it."

"Hm, well, never mind—it'll heal. I'm glad that man's gone. Good riddance! But I bet he'll get married the moment he gets back to wherever he's going."

"And why not? You're getting married too, aren't you?"

"Me? That's entirely different! What a funny man you are. If you're fifty, then he must be sixty! Anyway, ta-ta! Glad I bumped into you. Can't stay—don't ask me—no time!"

He started to leave but stopped abruptly and returned.

"Wait, what an idiot I am! I forgot—he asked me to give you this." Loboff handed him an envelope. "Why didn't you see him off yourself? Ta-ta!"

Loboff dashed off again, leaving Velchaninoff standing there. He returned home, sat down, and opened the letter. It was addressed to him and sealed, but inside, there was nothing written by Pavel Pavlovitch himself. Instead, he found another letter tucked inside—an old, yellowed piece of paper with faded ink.

He recognized the handwriting immediately. It was from Natalia Vasilievna, written ten years ago, shortly after he had left T——. He had never received this particular letter, though he remembered another one she had sent at the time. This one, however, was entirely different. In it, Natalia bade him farewell forever and informed him that she was expecting a child in a few months. She mentioned she would ensure he had the chance to meet the child one day and spoke of their bond as a friendship now "cemented forever." She also asked him to stop loving her, as she could no longer love him in return, but gave him permission to visit T—— after a year to see the child.

Velchaninoff sat frozen, pale as death, clutching the letter. He imagined Pavel Pavlovitch discovering it in the family's black wooden box with its mother-of-pearl inlays and silver trimmings. What must have gone through his mind as he read it for the first time?

"I bet he went as white as a sheet," Velchaninoff thought, catching sight of his own reflection in the mirror. "He probably stared at it, closed his eyes, and prayed that when he opened them, it would just be a blank piece of paper. Maybe he tried that two or three times before he finally accepted the truth."

Chapter 17

Two years had passed since the events described, and now Velchaninoff was sitting in a railway carriage on a beautiful summer day, heading toward Odessa. His trip had two purposes: to visit a close friend and to finally meet a woman whose acquaintance he had long wished to make.

Over the past two years, Velchaninoff had undergone a significant transformation. He was no longer the anxious, miserable man consumed by hypochondria. He had rejoined society, and his friends had welcomed him back with open arms, seemingly forgetting his period of isolation. Even acquaintances he had once avoided were now eager to rekindle their connections, treating his absence as if he had simply been away on private business.

His return to a brighter life was largely due to his success in resolving the legal matters previously troubling him and the security of having sixty thousand roubles safely tucked away at the bank. This newfound financial stability gave him a sense of confidence and vitality. His wrinkles had smoothed out, his eyes sparkled with life again, and his complexion was healthier. As he sat comfortably in the first-class carriage, he reflected on how much he had changed and felt almost like a new man.

The train was soon approaching a station where passengers would have forty minutes to dine. During the meal, Velchaninoff had the chance to assist a young woman in distress. She was pleasant-looking, though somewhat overdressed, and accompanied by a young officer who had clearly overindulged at the bar. The officer got into a heated argument with another equally inebriated man, and a scuffle broke out, threatening to spill over onto the young woman. Velchaninoff intervened, separating the two and restoring order. The lady was overwhelmed with gratitude, calling him her "guardian angel." She seemed to be a provincial woman, as evidenced by her somewhat unsophisticated manners and attire.

Their conversation revealed her frustrations about her absent husband, who had conveniently disappeared when he was most needed. "If you tell me his name, I'll help you find him," Velchaninoff offered politely.

"Pavel Pavlovitch," slurred the young officer nearby.

Velchaninoff's curiosity piqued at the name. "Your husband's name is Pavel Pavlovitch?" he asked, just as a familiar bald head appeared between him and the lady.

"Here you are at last!" the woman exclaimed hysterically.

Indeed, it was Pavel Pavlovitch. The moment he saw Velchaninoff, his face turned pale, and he recoiled as if he had seen a ghost. For a while, it seemed as though he couldn't comprehend his wife's explanation of how Velchaninoff had come to her aid or her scolding about his absence.

Finally, Pavel Pavlovitch seemed to recover from his shock. Velchaninoff burst into laughter. "Why, we're old friends!" he exclaimed, clapping Pavel on the shoulder in a friendly manner. Pavel managed a weak smile. "Haven't you ever mentioned me to your wife?"

"No, never," the woman admitted, somewhat embarrassed.

"Well, introduce me then, you faithless friend!" Velchaninoff teased.

"This is Mr. Velchaninoff," Pavel muttered awkwardly.

With the tension broken, the mood lightened, and Pavel was sent off to fetch refreshments. Meanwhile, his wife explained to

Velchaninoff that they were traveling from O——, where Pavel worked, to their country home about twenty-five miles away. She invited Velchaninoff to visit them, expressing her gratitude and promising to make his stay enjoyable. Velchaninoff, always the charmer, replied that he would be delighted, adding a few compliments that made her blush.

When Pavel returned, his wife informed him that Velchaninoff had agreed to visit them for a month. Pavel's face betrayed his dismay, though he managed a feeble smile and said nothing.

After dinner, as Pavel and his wife returned to their carriage, Velchaninoff stayed behind, strolling the platform with a cigar. He knew Pavel would return to speak with him, and sure enough, he did.

"So, you're coming to visit us?" Pavel began nervously.

"I knew you'd start with that! You haven't changed a bit," Velchaninoff replied, laughing heartily. "Do you really think I'd stay with you for a month? Don't be absurd."

Pavel looked relieved. "You're not coming, then?" he asked, unable to hide his joy.

"No, of course not," Velchaninoff said, still laughing. For some reason, the entire situation struck him as hilariously absurd.

"But my wife thinks you're coming!" Pavel said, distressed.

"Tell her I broke my leg or something," Velchaninoff suggested, laughing harder.

"She won't believe me," Pavel muttered anxiously.

As the second bell rang, Pavel prepared to leave, but Velchaninoff stopped him. "Shall I tell her how you tried to cut my throat?" he asked sharply.

Pavel froze in terror. "God forbid!" he stammered.

"Then go!" Velchaninoff said, releasing him.

As the train whistle blew and Pavel began to board, Velchaninoff seized him by the shoulder. His tone turned cold. "If I can offer you my hand after everything"—he showed the scar on his palm—"the least you can do is accept it."

Pavel's face turned ghostly white, his lips trembling. "And—Liza?" he whispered, his voice breaking as tears filled his eyes.

Velchaninoff stood motionless, his anger and pity warring within him.

"Pavel Pavlovitch! Hurry!" his wife's desperate voice called from the train.

Pavel hesitated, then scrambled onto the moving train. Velchaninoff watched as it disappeared into the distance. Moments later, he boarded the next train, continuing his journey to Odessa.

THE END

Thank you for Reading

You've Just Read a Piece of the Greatest Library Ever Rebuilt

Thank you for reading.

This book is one of thousands we're restoring, reimagining, and translating as part of the **Modern Library of Alexandria** — a global movement to preserve and share humanity's most important ideas.

What was once lost to fire and time is now rising again — not just as memory, but as living, breathing knowledge, freely accessible to all.

What You Can Do Next:

- **Keep Reading.**

   Discover more legendary works — in beautiful print, audiobook, or digital form — at LibraryofAlexandria.com.

- **Build Your Own Library.**

   Every title is available as a paperback, hardcover, or collectible boxset — at true printing cost. Craft a personal library worthy of display.

- **Spread the Light.**

   Share this book. Tell others about the movement. Help us translate every timeless work into every language, so no reader is ever left behind.

By finishing this book, you've already taken part in something extraordinary.

Join us at LibraryofAlexandria.com

Together, we're rebuilding the greatest library the world has ever known.

With appreciation,
The Modern Library of Alexandria Team

Visit:

www.libraryofalexandria.com

Or scan the code below:

www.ingramcontent.com/pod-product-compliance
Lightning Source LLC
Chambersburg PA
CBHW011203090426
42742CB00019B/3397